the Unexplained

Great Mysteries of the 20th Century

JENNY RANDLES

Anaya Publishers Ltd

LONDON

First published in Great Britain in 1994 by
Anaya Publishers Limited 3rd Floor, Strode House
44-50 Osnaburgh Street London NW1 3ND

British Library Cataloguing in Publication Data

Randles, Jenny
The Unexplained: Great Mysteries of the 20th Century
    I. Title
    001.9

ISBN 1-85470-178-9 (hardback only)
ISBN 1-85470-086-3 (paperback only)

Designed by Glynn Pickerill
Design Production by The R & B Partnership
Edited by John Gilbert
Printed and bound in Portugal

Cover photographs by Fortean Picture Library
Frontispiece, of a medium producing ectoplasm in a
1920 experiment, by Fortean Picture Library

CONTENTS

INTRODUCTION

During the twentieth century the strangest things have happened both in the worlds of science and of parascience.

So-called normal science has witnessed a revolution so immense as to equal or even surpass those pioneered by Newton and Galileo. We have reached upward and outward into space, probed the interior of the atom, discovered hidden radiations, revealed a ghost universe filled with time-travelling phantoms and created technological miracles unforeseen even by the writers of science fiction. The sinister side to these achievements is the unleashing of natural catastrophes and the forging of weapons capable of ending life on Earth. No single century in history can match this record of inventiveness, with its unlimited potential for creation and destruction.

In the wake of this galloping charge by the forces of rationalism has come a deluge of paranormal phenomena that seems to herald a return to the distant age of superstition. We have been asked to believe in fairies and spacemen, we have sought for meaning

Drawing of the 'Jersey Devil', *Philadelphia Evening Bulletin*, January 1909.

in past lives and we have used computers to probe the future. Our oceans have teemed with monsters, our fields have been speckled with mysterious circles and our skies have been overflown by dazzling fleets of UFOs.

It seems appropriate, as the century draws to a close, to review the logbook of the last hundred years, examining some of these remarkable events and developments to see how things may inter-relate.

To this end I have devised a chronology of ten most extraordinary decades, describing many of the broad trends and individual mysteries that have paralleled, and often outstripped, the realities of fact and the fantasies of fiction. They have woven their way, like an invisible thread, through the annals of this fascinating period to create a tapestry of awesome beauty, outshining anything in the pages of the *Arabian Nights*.

So climb aboard our magic carpet for a ride through the twentieth century. Who knows what wonders we shall confront?

Sir John Hunt leading the Everest expedition of 1953. The Himalayas have been the scene of several alleged sightings of the Abominable Snowman.

THE NEW CENTURY

As the twentieth century dawned, thanks to Darwin's theory of evolution, the birth of psychoanalysis as pioneered by Sigmund Freud and the experimental research of Anton Pavlov, science seemed close to creating an ordered, predictable world peopled by automata: a godless Universe with no spirit, no soul and no afterlife.

More encouraging were the first faltering steps into a gravity-free environment as scientists and aviators converted age-old dreams into reality.

Yet, as traditional religion declined, the human spirit rebelled, creating new modes of expression for its inner world, as if to prove to science that all was not quite as simple as it seemed.

1900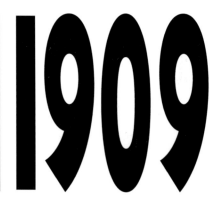

1900 14 FEBRUARY

THE VANISHING AT HANGING ROCK

One of the most astonishing disappearances on record took place at Hanging Rock, near Melbourne, Victoria, Australia. This was recorded in the book *Picnic at Hanging Rock* by Joan Lindsay (1967), and was also the subject of an ethereal and eerie 1975 film of the same title by Peter Weir. The book, although labelled a novel, is by implication based on fact. It tells of a school party on a day outing at the isolated beauty spot, and how four teenage girls and a female teacher vanished after setting off, in sight of many colleagues, to explore a rock face in the bush. One girl returned in a state of deep shock. Another, in an equally catatonic condition, was found a week later. Neither could explain what had occurred. The three missing members of the party were never found. A strange pink cloud seen hovering near by reinforced the supernatural view that they had slipped into another dimension or time. The event struck a chord deep in the psyche because of its direct challenge to scientific omnipotence. On the other hand, whereas many of the people and places did historically exist, the Joan Lindsay novel contains serious errors of fact and no contemporary media accounts refer to the vanishings. When asked in 1977 if she had invented it all, the author replied, enigmatically, that this was impossible to answer because 'fact and fiction are so closely intertwined'.

1900 MID-DECEMBER

THE LIGHTHOUSE DISAPPEARANCE

On 6 December, Joseph Moore left for three weeks' leave from the desolate Eilean Mor lighthouse on the Flannan Isles, west of Lewis, Scotland. When he returned on Boxing Day, the three men left in charge had vanished. No weapons had been touched and there was no trace of a disturbance. The last log entry by the men, dated 15 December, referred to the calmness of the sea after the ending of a strange storm not recorded twenty miles away, and mentioned that they were afraid, praying and affirming that 'God is over all'.

1901 JUNE

AN EARLY CLOSE ENCOUNTER

The first recorded close encounter of the third kind (or alien contact) occurred at Bournbrook, West Midlands, England, when an object like a 'hut' was seen in a garden by a youth. It contained two small men, under 4 feet tall, wearing khaki suits and helmets, one of whom approached the witness before returning inside. The object created an electrical glow around its base and took off skyward with a whooshing noise.

1901 10 AUGUST

TIMESLIP AT VERSAILLES

Two English schoolteachers, Anne Moberley and Eleanor Jourdain, were on holiday in France. Visiting the grounds of the Palace of Versailles on a hot sunny day, they claimed to have been projected more than a century back in time. They came across the Petit Trianon, the small château given by Louis XVI to Marie-Antoinette, as it had been on 10 August 1792, the historic day when the French royal family was forced to flee. The two women wandered pathways that no longer existed, saw people in old-fashioned clothing and even witnessed a woman busy painting who stared them full in the face and bore the resemblance of Marie-Antoinette herself. Only following later visits to the scene,

Above: the Petit Trianon, Versailles.
Below: Eleanor Jourdain and Anne Moberley

when they noted that pathways they had trodden in 1901 had since vanished, and when subsequently researching the history of the grounds, did they come to understand many of these events.

The women stood by their story until their deaths, despite sceptical claims that they had stumbled across a costume party (the existence of which was never verified). They described a flat feel to the imagery and other strange sensations typical of more recent slips through time; and some modern researchers think this is indeed what happened. Somehow they slid through the years or 'tuned into' a memory left by the Queen in the grounds of the château.

1902

TRIUMPH OF THE SPIRIT

As the century began, mysterious events such as these confirmed the view of many ordinary people that science was mistaken to presume that all things could be resolved. The scientific desire to prove the soul redundant was matched by the increasing belief in Spiritualism.

This movement had begun in the eastern United States after simple messages, believed to come from beyond the grave, were received by the controversial Fox sisters in Hydesville, New York. The belief that the dead were in another dimension and that contact with them was possible spawned both religious institutions and the Society for Psychical Research. The latter, based in London, aimed to persuade scientists to study such reports, and like its religious counterpart, it was soon to spread around the world.

The religion of spirit messages, with preachers known as mediums, proliferated in the 1890s and was legally constituted into the Spiritualists' National Union in 1902. The appeal of the movement gained momentum and remained constant throughout the rest of the century. The slaughter of world wars and countless bloody local conflicts brought many bereaved rushing to Spiritualist churches for comfort.

The real reason for this success was that, while conventional religions called for faith as a path toward solace, they had no way of combating the advance of science. Indeed, some sects broke away and attempted to bring back a puritanical way of life and to restore literal belief in the truth of the Old Testament stories that had by now been severely eroded by rationalism. On the other hand, Spiritualism offered hard evidence, albeit in the guise of mediums passing on often vague tittle-tattle about dead relatives and friends. But for many that was sufficiently persuasive.

The only answer science had was to cry 'cheat' and, often without any proof of this assumption, to argue that people were deluding themselves. Thus, at one and the same time, Spiritualism established a barrier that science, with all its might, could barely dent; and it offered hope to a world fast being stripped to its spiritual bones.

Inevitably, as a consequence of this and the maxim that one could fool some people most of the time, charlatans cashed in. Phoney mediums sprang up all over the place. The new gadgetry of science, from photography to X-ray tubes, was hi-jacked for 'experiments' in which dubious spirit images, floating clouds of ectoplasm (the transient 'matter' of the spirit world) and other such doubtful practices became rife.

It was some time before Spiritualism was able to set its own house in order and as a consequence a growing rift developed between the popular believers and the scientific sceptics, who accused these gullible folk of believing only because they wanted to and not because the evidence dictated it. This rift widened as the century progressed.

Nowadays, Spiritualism has waned slightly, but it has also become big business, thanks to the instant celebrity status afforded by TV. Doris Stokes, Doris Collins, Stephen O'Brien and many others have brought their ministrations to the world, packing venues such as the Sydney Opera House, theatres in London's West End, etc., and drawing in enormous ratings for the media. In response, scientific vigilante groups such as CSICOP (Committee for the Scientific Investigation of Claims of the Paranormal) have launched themselves as guardians of rationalism, sniping away on the fringes of the supernatural, bringing down the occasional victim, but largely failing to penetrate the armour of hope and belief that Spiritualism provides for so many.

As to whether it is truth or delusion, like all spiritual matters throughout history, that question remains a matter of faith.

1904 SEPTEMBER

THE LEAPING MONSTER

Spring-heeled Jack was a bizarre creature often reported in Victorian London during the nineteenth century. He had grown to legendary status. With his grotesque face, and clad in a black cape, he would apparently leap out of nowhere and attack people in the streets, often leaving them wounded though not dead. His name derived from his reputed ability to jump huge distances in one bound. Although there were isolated sightings in London even after World War Two, the last prominent one was in Liverpool in 1904 when the figure was said to have jumped over a building in William Henry Street. However, research by sceptic Paul Begg revealed this as an exaggeration of a true story of a religious zealot who claimed the devil was chasing him and who leapt dangerously from rooftop to rooftop to escape the attentions of the police and fire services. Legend has associated this spuriously with a manifestation of the archetypal Victorian monster.

Above and opposite: two imaginative popular renderings, from 1877 and 1904, of Spring-heeled Jack.

1905 JANUARY

THE BINBROOK POLTERGEIST

One of the most frightening poltergeist outbreaks struck Binbrook Farm, in Lincolnshire, England. Objects moved around the room on their own, hundreds of chickens were found skinned and slaughtered noiselessly even after a guard had been mounted, and mysterious fires sprang up from nowhere. In one case a teenage ser-

ONE PENNY

② SPRING-HEELED JACK

A MYSTERY OF MYSTERIES

On the tombstone, with upraised arms and rage in every feature,
towered the terrific form of Spring-Heeled Jack. Freezer and Links
stood transfixed; their ghastly burden slipped slowly to the grass,
but they remained gaping, terror-struck. Vengeance had fallen!

vant caught ablaze as she was sweeping the floor and was hospitalized with serious injuries. The incidents lasted two months and then ceased as rapidly as they began. The case became a prototype for future attacks of this nature the world over. Opinion at first was that 'evil spirits' were to blame, but this altered later to the para-scientific theory that some unknown but latent energy within a traumatized victim 'leaked' out and was somehow translated into destructive physical force. Science maintains that such cases are mere coincidence or fabrication.

1905 JANUARY

LIGHTS OF INSPIRATION

Egryn is a small village north of Barmouth on the mid-Wales coast. In 1905 it became the centre of a traditional Methodist religious revival that was dramatically stimulated by a farmer's wife named Mary Jones. The principal reason for her astonishing achievements was the manner in which strange light phenomena attached themselves to her person. Hundreds of people saw them and her fame soon spread. The tiny chapel became a focal point for pilgrims.

The lights were first witnessed by a train driver at Pensarn in early January at a time when Mrs Jones was preaching in the town. He said they resembled glowing balls of fire that streaked away in many directions, then converged with a tremendous explosion like thunder. Another person described a bright blue bar that straddled a pitch-dark country road. And many witnesses claimed to have seen the lights hovering directly over Mary Jones and inside churches where she preached.

There followed six months of dazzling light shows in the skies that brought journalists scurrying from as far afield as London and Manchester. These were dramatically concluded on 23 July when a ball

of fire sent down two feelers toward the ground at Ynysybwl.

It was argued that some of the lights were probably misperceptions of the planet Venus, then bright in the night sky, or meteor activity, which was little understood at the time. In any event, the mysterious lights helped Mary Jones to circulate her religious message, and when they finally disappeared, her influence declined.

Kevin McClure conducted detailed research into the matter and regards the phenomenon as an important phase in the development of religious visions – strong in Catholic communities of Ireland, France and Spain, but rare outside. Modern researchers, however, think that these lights may be produced by the ground itself. Rocks are known to generate electrical signals when put under strain, e.g. during earthquakes. Short-lived glowing plasmas seem to be created in the atmosphere as a result of this fault line activity. In the years prior to the Welsh revival, they were termed 'spooklights'. Today, of course, the same lights would be seen as UFOs.

Researcher Paul Devereux has coined the term 'earthlight' to define these glows and has found a fault line running right past the Egryn church.

1908 30 JUNE

THE TUNGUSKA SKY CRASH

An earthlight to end all earthlights was seen by remote villagers in the Siberian taiga forest near the Stony Tunguska River. Its origin remains the subject of intense controversy but its impact is beyond dispute.

Shortly after 7 a.m. that morning, a white mass, brighter than the sun, appeared in the sky above northern Europe, creating ground shadows. Within seconds it swept across the desolate landscape miles high in the atmosphere and turned into a column climbing vertically upward and visible for hundreds of miles around. There followed a series of huge explosions which were heard sixty miles from the impact point.

Minutes after the event, a shock wave spread outward. It uprooted trees and smashed rooftops more than seventy miles from the centre of destruction. It was felt as an earth tremor in Germany and recorded even in Britain. Measured on widely dispersed seismographs, the wave was powerful enough to circle the Earth – twice!

For several subsequent nights strange luminous clouds lit the skies above Europe and Africa. They glowed pink and yellow and were bright enough for people to read newspapers outdoors in the absence of any artificial lighting.

Because of the remoteness of the impact zone and the intervention of the Russian revolution it was almost twenty years before a scientific expedition reached Tunguska. Astronomer Leonard Kulik expected to find evidence of a meteor that had exploded on impact, leaving a huge crater and fragments behind. In fact, he found neither crater nor fragments. Trees at the exact centre of the explosion, although stripped of bark, were still standing; those in a surrounding area many miles across were flattened.

The meteorite theory was all but destroyed by this evidence, which clearly showed that the object had exploded high in mid-air, so that the area immediately below was to some extent shielded. There were also reports by local foresters that the glowing mass had seemed to change direction in mid-flight – a fact partially vindicated, despite much argument, by aerodynamic reconstruction.

Scientists now favour the view that the object was a small comet. To create an impact of a 12-megatonne nuclear bomb, as this object had done, it would need to be several hundred feet in diameter, far bigger than a meteor.

Comets are composed of a solid crumbly core and ice that vaporizes in a shell on the outside. This produces the characteristic comet's tail. If a piece of comet had hit the Earth, it would have largely vaporized and sprinkled fine dust over the ground. Locals indeed referred to a black rain that accompanied the Tunguska impact. Particles of dust thrown into the atmosphere could also have produced the luminous clouds.

Nevertheless, after nuclear weapons were first detonated in 1945 and their effects were seen to be remarkably similar to those in Siberia, a popular parascience theory emerged. Was the Tunguska explosion the result of a nuclear-powered spacecraft that exploded on its way into the atmosphere?

Supporters pointed out that local reindeer developed scabs on their bodies and there was some limited evidence for excessive radiation in the area (although measured only following man-made nuclear detonations by the USSR, which compromised the findings). Kulik had found no local people who suffered radiation sickness on his visit in 1928; and by 1940, when he went again, direct eyewitnesses to the event were still found alive and well – improbable had they been very close observers to a nuclear impact.

Several more recent expeditions have found evidence consistent with the comet theory, including elements and chemicals on the ground. A precise mapping of the impact damage also fits the idea. However, other Russian scientists who have visited the area think that something unexplained was to blame. Theories as diverse as a lump of anti-matter exploding on contact with the atmosphere, and even a nuclear-powered space rocket from the future which accidentally crossed a time barrier and then detonated, have been proposed, but without much foundation.

Yet if the Tunguska explosion was caused by an impact from a piece of debris from outer space, one thing is certain. Such a happening is not all that rare and may be expected by chance every few hundred years. Smaller ones will occur several times a century. It would have been pure luck

15

9TH AND ARCH MUSEUM

T. F. HOPKINS..............Manager

CAUGHT!!! AND HERE!!! ALIVE!!!

THE

LEEDS DEVIL
Captured Friday After a Terrific Struggle

EXHIBITED EXCLUSIVELY HERE AT $1000.00 A WEEK.
The Fearful, Frightful, Ferocious Monster Which Has Been Terrorizing Two States.

Swims! Flys! Gallops!

Exhibited Securely Chained In a Massive Steel Cage.

A LIVING DRAGON

More Fearsome Than the Fabled Monsters of Mythology.
DON'T MISS THE SIGHT OF A LIFETIME.

BIG STRING OF SENSATIONS IN CURIO HALL

THEATRE
GRAND CONTINUOUS VAUDEVILLE

10¢ ADMITS TO ALL

---

that the 1908 object exploded over a relatively uninhabited area. The next one could just as easily do so over London, Tokyo or the heart of Manhattan, with all too obvious consequences.

1909 17 JANUARY

THE JERSEY DEVIL

For a week the small communities of New Jersey, USA, were plagued with sightings of a giant bat-like creature with a face that was likened variously to a mule, a dog or a kangaroo. It was said to be terrorizing local farms, landing, leaving strange marks and then leaping into the sky.

The prints were in the form of a single hoof and seemed to pass straight over obstacles such as fences. They were also found on beaches in deep snow.

In many ways the tracks resembled those left in the still mysterious incident in February 1855 when residents of villages over a large area of South Devon awoke one morning to find a line of single hoofprints etched into a snowdrift. It spread for many miles over the landscape and even crossed rooftops as if unimpeded!

In 1909 reports began on 17 January when a policeman shot at the thing as it flew over the Delaware River in Pennsylvania. Sounds like a shrieking whistle were heard. On 21 January firemen at West Collingswood, New Jersey, were reputedly attacked by the 3-foot monster with glowing eyes. It then perched on a roof and they turned their hoses on to it, to its apparent disgust! In New Jersey, the sightings of the creature in conjunction with the finding of the hoofprints soon gave rise to hysteria, and the name 'Jersey Devil' was coined, from a local legend

The wave ended with reports from Morrisville, Pennsylvania, that the creature had

A poster in the *Philadelphia Public Ledger* of a precursor to the Jersey Devil, this one exhibited in captivity.

flown into a barn and become trapped. The doors were sealed and reinforcements rapidly sent for. Unfortunately, when the barn doors were opened, and despite there being no other obvious exit route, the Jersey Devil had vanished into the hinter-world from which it had arrived and was never heard from again.

At least, not until 1966, when Ohio had a terrifying spate of visions of a creature possessing a number of similar features that became known as 'mothman'.

1909

PHANTOM SCARESHIPS

As the first primitive aircraft were flying on dangerous short hops around the world, the inexplicable appearance of a wave of strange airships soon developed into a mystery of epic proportions.

The first flight by a Zeppelin; LZ-1, over Lake Constance, Germany, 2 July 1900.

In fact, the first sighting occurred in the autumn of 1896, in Sacramento and later San Francisco, California, when a cigar-shaped object with bright lights was reported floating in the air. According to research by Jerome Clark, frontier humour had a field day. As the sightings continued almost nightly, many tall tales were spun simply to outdo rival provincial papers. Eccentric inventors came forward to claim, through agents, that they had built the devices, then vanished without ever making public their secret.

A further outbreak was reported across a wider area of the western and mid-western states in April and May 1897. The first flights by genuine airships – which began in Europe – were still some months away. But, like the previous wave, the 1897 airships of the western USA swiftly disappeared.

In 1909, however, the problem suddenly became global, as scattered reports came in from New Zealand, Australia and especially from Britain.

On 23 March, a policeman on patrol in Peterborough, north-east of Cambridge, heard a buzzing engine and looked up to see a single floodlight attached to a dark cigar-shape silhouetted against the sky. Local police suggested it was an illuminated kite, but as more reports followed, rumour spread that the Germans were flying Zeppelins on spy missions. There was real tension between the two imperial nations in the run-up to World War One; but although the activities of airship builder Count Ferdinand von Zeppelin were well attested, it is certain that no such spy missions were ever launched against Britain in this way, nor did the Germans have the capability to do so.

On 14 May, the captain and crew of the *St Olaf*, steaming in the North Sea off Blyth, Northumberland, saw an object apparently materialize out of thin air above. It was again described as a cigar with lights.

An even more remarkable incident took place on 18 May which has all the hallmarks of a UFO landing. If it were reported today, few details would need to be adjusted for it to be interpreted as an alien contact, rather than – as it was at the time – a precursor to a German invasion.

Punch and Judy showman, Mr C. Lethbridge, was walking home late at night over Caerphilly Mountain in South Wales when he saw a cigar-like object on the ground. Two men wearing strange fur coats were talking in an unknown language and reacted instinctively when they saw the intruder, picking up something from the ground and jumping into their craft, which soared skyward over some telegraph wires. As it rose, two powerful searchlight beams were switched on, one at each end of the craft.

The witness returned to the site with friends to find objects on the grass, including a piece of blue paper with unknown writing and printed matter about the

German army! The terrain was also crushed flat.

There were other reports of airship pilots standing beside their craft, in one case requesting water. But after a few days the sightings tailed off, leaving the usual speculation about mistaken identity and mass hysteria.

The sightings began again, however, in late 1912. One incident, above Sheerness, Kent, on 14 October, was then taken so seriously that questions were asked in the House of Commons – possibly the first ever public debate on UFOs. Lord of the Admiralty and future prime minister, Winston Churchill, had the dubious privilege of being the first government official under

Trial flight of the Zeppelin LZ-4 over Lake Constance, 1908.

pressure to come up with an answer and warned of the need not to underestimate the German forces. A law was passed that prohibited airship flights without prior authority and allowed the police or army to shoot one down if it failed to respond to warning signals. No such incident, fortunately, occurred.

The final fling of these airship waves before war erupted came on the night of 21 February 1913 when reports flooded in from several parts of Britain. Most interesting was one from the small village of Exhall in Warwickshire. It was just a typical description of a lighted object, but was to acquire more relevance because the same location has since generated several fascinat-

ing light-in-the-sky phenomena not viewed as airships. One, on 30 December 1977, involved a golden egg shape seen rising from power lines, punching a hole in the cloud cover which then gradually filled in until no longer visible.

Modern researchers suspect that there is some sort of natural phenomenon of a glowing, electrical nature, possibly akin to Devereux's earthlights. When seen in 1977, the ionization caused the clouds to disperse. Today we understandably view these things as alien craft, but in 1909 and 1913, immersed in pre-war hysteria, were they seen as scareships?

PORTENTS OF WAR

This traumatic decade, punctured by rebellion and revolution, culminated in the titanic and bloody clash of World War One, the 'war to end all wars'.

Meanwhile the scientific revolution gathered momentum. Albert Einstein's 'general theory' of relativity turned our notion of the Universe on its head. The form taken by basic conceptions such as speed, size, shape and time was relative to where you were and what you were doing. Atoms were composed of energy fields in constant flux within largely empty space, beyond the grasp of our normal senses. New vistas opened up, ready for exploration. The Universe had suddenly become a vastly more complicated place.

1910  1919

MIRACLE BLEEDING

This was one of the first well-attested reports of miracle bleedings. A picture of Christ in the French village church at Mire-beau-en-Poitou began to ooze blood from the hands and the forehead. While scientists argued that it was just pigmentation from the paint seeping out, the devout flocked to the site, convinced that the local priest was somehow responsible. The location of the bleedings was exactly that of the reputed wounds of Christ when crucified, i.e. on the hands and crown. Yet, interestingly, the hands bled at the centre point, long believed to be where nails were placed during crucifixion and familiar from many religious portraits. We now know from historical evidence, however, that crucifixion victims had nails hammered through the bones at the wrist as the fleshy palm was too soft to support the hanging weight of a body. The bleeding intensified for six months and at the same time a nearby statue of the Virgin 'wept' tears. After the priest's death in 1915 all these effects ceased.

15. September 1911.

15 Septembre 1911

Dezember 1911.

Décembre 1911

21

PREMONITION OF DISASTER

The *Titanic*, built in the northern English port of Liverpool and steaming from Southampton to New York, is probably the most infamous name in marine history. Several days into her maiden voyage, the so-called 'unsinkable' liner struck an unseen iceberg, was holed deep and carried 1500 passengers and crew to the bottom of the Atlantic Ocean. More people would have been saved from her huge contingent had not the owners, utterly convinced of her security, neglected to provide enough lifeboats.

A side effect of the shocking disaster was to set in motion one of the most powerful psychic experiences ever recorded. For the first time there was open talk of precognition – the ability to see things before they happen.

No fewer than twenty cases are known of people who had premonitions of disaster before the ship sailed. Some refused to board; others had relatives among the passengers and sensed tragedy. Famed newspaper writer William Stead, who had himself written in an article that such a tragedy could happen, was warned explicitly in writing by a psychic that he was in great danger during April 1912 and should avoid water and travel at that time. He ignored the warning and paid with his life.

Even more incredible was the case of retired seaman Morgan Robertson who was struggling to sell his short stories. In 1898, experiencing writer's block in his New York apartment, he suddenly had a vision in which he saw a huge liner suffer a catastrophe with an iceberg. In his trance, he heard clearly the words 'April' and 'unsinkable'.

Inspired by this episode, he wrote his story 'The Wreck of the Titan', in which his near-identical supership, the SS *Titan*, sinks on her maiden voyage after striking an

unseen iceberg, with hundreds perishing needlessly because of inadequate lifeboat cover.

Sceptics argued that this was mere coincidence. Former seamen may understandably have had qualms about the safety of such a big liner. Moreover, *Titan* or *Titanic* was an obvious choice of name for a huge ship. Yet Robertson felt sure he had an unseen presence guiding his hand. Or could it genuinely have been precognition?

Left: survivors packing the Titanic lifeboats.
Below: the last moments of the 'unsinkable' liner.

CRETACEOUS PARK

Sir Arthur Conan Doyle's fiction of surviving dinosaurs had real-life inspiration from legends and stories first brought back by eighteenth-century missionaries from the African Congo. Then, in late 1913, the German government sent out the first scientific expedition to ascertain the likely truth behind these tales.

Captain Freiherr von Stein set out on a long and treacherous walk through the jungle swamps of the Likoula region, encountering venomous snakes, deadly insects and headhunting pygmies as he ventured into uncharted territory situated hundreds of miles from any towns or cities. After questioning natives and white hunters who had explored the region, he repeatedly heard legends about a large beast, some 20-30 ft long, which inhabited a local lake.

The creature, named *mokele mbembe*, was said to have a long neck and brown body and to be bigger than a hippopotamus. It lived in the lake caves and surfaced periodically to eat leaves from a flowering liana plant called *molombo*, stretching its neck upward rather like a giraffe. Natives who had approached the animal in canoes had been attacked and drowned when their boats sank, but there were no claims that the monster ate its prey.

Von Stein never saw the creature but was shown a track by natives who swore that a specimen had recently entered the river system at that point. He could add little except that the animal which left the marks was about the size that had been described and unfamiliar to him.

The general view of zoologists was that the legends might have had a factual basis, particularly because the creature was not depicted as a terrifying or carnivorous beast (as is normal with such stories) but described as a placid plant eater. Herbivorous dinosaurs such as *Brontosaurus* flourished in the Cretaceous era and it was just conceivable that a few specimens still sur-

Skeletal model of *Diplodocus*, the Cretaceous dinosaur.

vived locally. But in the absence of proof, nobody seemed inclined to be too excited by a collection of stories.

Subsequent attempts to mount dinosaur hunts failed because of hostile natives. In the 1940s, however, a new field of research was launched by a group of professionals who called themselves 'cryptozoologists'. They collected data and tried to create public interest by searching for hidden creatures such as *mokele mbembe*. In 1958, one of their number, Bernard Heuvelmans, published the first detailed accounts in 'On the Track of Unknown Animals'.

During the 1970s an American specialist in reptiles visited the area several times and showed illustrations of dinosaurs to a recent eyewitness of the creature, who picked out a *Diplodocus* as the most similar one.

The first serious expeditions specifically designed to find the animal were organized by Professor Roy Mackal, a biologist at the University of Chicago, with the reptile specialist, James Powell. Mackal mounted several more visits before the new Congolese

government put difficulties in the way. These trips established much useful data, assembling matching accounts and reports of how in 1959 a group of pygmies captured and ate one of the creatures. But the scientists only had tantalizing near misses, as when one huge lumbering beast splashed into the water just out of sight.

American explorer Herman Regusters visited in the 1980s and his party claimed to see the creature several times and hear its throaty roar. They took some dim, distant pictures through the dense tree cover.

Local scientist Dr Marcellin Agnaga, from the zoological gardens in Brazzaville, also made several visits and in May 1983 came closest yet to capturing proof when he wandered out into the shallows to come within a few hundred feet of a basking *mokele mbembe*. For half an hour the animal browsed on liana leaves before sinking beneath the water. Sadly, through a combination of human error, misfortune and the extreme climate, none of his photographs survived the trek home.

The Japanese have since tried twice, and a young British ex-army man, Bill Gibbons,

Dinosaur and human tracks in Dinosaur Valley State Park, Glen Rose, Texas. (See also page 39.)

has been there two more times (most recently in 1992) in what has been dubbed 'Operation Congo'. This was supported by a paranormal magazine which sold dinosaur T-shirts to raise funds!

Much anecdotal evidence has been gathered and latest thinking is that the creature is an evolved version of *Atlantosaurus*. Such dinosaurs did live in these swamps during the late Cretaceous geological period some sixty-five million years ago and the area has remained almost unaltered.

It is perhaps feasible that a few such creatures may have survived in this remote region. But as Western society intrudes ever further into Africa, they are bound to come under threat. It may be a race against extinction to come up with hard evidence about the world's last surviving dinosaurs.

13 MAY

THE TESTAMENT OF PATIENCE WORTH

On this date Pearl Curran and a friend, using a ouija board in the Curran home at St Louis, Missouri, first saw the name 'Pat C' spelt out by the moving glass. Pearl's husband, determined to prove the incoming message a trick of the mind, pretended he had once known an Irishman named Pat. For a time that fictitious individual sent messages via the board, but soon a new and more powerful voice took control. On 8 July, the cryptic words that flowed out whenever Pearl Curran used the device were explicitly signed 'Patience Worth'.

Patience, belying her name, soon outgrew the slow ouija board, graduating first to automatic writing; pen in hand, she would 'take over' Mrs Curran and write lengthy scripts, and finally took to sending words straight into the consciousness of her medium.

It required some effort to extract information about herself from Patience. She was reportedly a Quaker girl who emigrated from Dorset to the USA in the seventeenth century and died young during an Indian attack. She spoke in archaic language, complete with spelling and usages that linguistic scholars verified as being totally correct. Later, however, she began to utilize a more modern idiom.

Patience Worth seems to have expressed herself freely in literary form. Across twenty-five years she came up with millions of words, including widely acclaimed novels, plays and poems, some of which were published without reference to their bizarre creation. Patience 'dictated' them with astonishing rapidity. Once, when asked for a motto of about 120 characters to put on the wall of the Missouri state capital, she drafted a literary ode of exactly the required length, in the brief time it took for Pearl Curran to write down the words. And the novels involved extraordinary depth of research knowledge about distant and future times – from the Biblical era to Victorian London.

Prior to her encounter with Patience, Mrs Curran's writings had exhibited no hint of sophistication or skill; and after she died, Patience fell silent, leaving behind the mystery of her highly praised literary genius.

So was this a real contact from a departed spirit or did Pearl Curran tap some hidden creative source from which great writers have long derived inspiration?

Automatic writers today continue the trend. Rosemary Brown, a London housewife, writes music that she says is dictated by dead composers such as Beethoven and Liszt. Healer Matthew Manning has created fabulous paintings in the style of artists such as Dürer and Picasso. A woman in the USA has informed me that she is currently seeking an agent to market the autobiography of Billy the Kid, determined to correct the false image of his outlaw days from beyond the grave. I have also received tapes from a New York medium, Bill Tenuto, containing verbal messages about the real purpose of his murder spoken by former Beatle, John Lennon. Mr Tenuto also reports that Lennon is dictating new music to some world renowned song writers.

1914

WONDERS OF WORLD WAR ONE

The first major battle of the war was fought at Mons in Flanders in August 1914. Legend has it that spectral intervention may have saved the day for the Allies.

British troops made a Dunkirk-style withdrawal against all the odds and a vastly superior German army. Although there were sound reasons as to why this was possible (the British had better weapons and highly disciplined soldiers), the victory from the jaws of defeat was hailed as a mir-

A corner of the ANZAC position at Gallipoli, scene of the ill-fated Allied landing of April 1915.

acle by politicians keen to rally the troops and the nation after what had almost been a catastrophe.

A few weeks later (in late September) the London *Evening News* carried a short piece of fiction by Arthur Machen called 'The Bowmen' in which a soldier at Mons invokes the spirit of St George, believed to ride to the rescue of England whenever she is in peril. The saint and a host of angelic bowmen reinforce the desperate Allies and the Germans are heavily felled by magical arrows that leave no marks.

The tale had a great effect on British morale. It was reprinted, often by church journals, as proof of divine support of the war, and soon became taken for fact. Eventually a special booklet was produced to satisfy demand.

Apparently Machen never pretended he

had done anything other than invent a tale. Indeed, when asked to quote his sources, he explained that there were none as it was untrue. But by then some people were so taken in by the account, they refused to believe Machen's denials!

In 1915 the story was procured by all manner of bodies, religious and military alike. Witnesses, usually second-hand, came forward with tales they had heard from 'men at the front' and eventually actual eye-witness accounts surfaced from soldiers claiming to have seen the phantom bowmen.

In July 1915 Machen fuelled the fire by producing a book, *The Bowmen and Other Legends of the War*. He described how his

27

fiction had become accepted as fact and reaffirmed that it was no more than a story. Yet it did not prevent the book becoming a runaway best-seller in many countries, doubtless with many readers believing the author's disavowal to be the real fiction.

By the end of the war the legend had become so entwined that some psychic authorities even alleged that Machen had 'tuned into' real witnesses to the vision at the Front, using telepathy directly from the troops at Mons. He only thought that he had invented the story. It was really true!

Later in the war, another strange event occurred which, like the bowmen at Mons, still holds sway today. This did, at least, have some factual basis in war records.

It surfaced in 1965 when an old soldier at a fiftieth reunion of the New Zealand and Australian troops involved in the Gallipoli campaign came forward. Sapper Frederick Reichardt and two others told on affidavit how on 21 August 1915 an entire regiment (the First-Fourth Norfolks) was seen to march towards Hill 60 above the hot deserted Suvla Bay area of the Dardanelles in Turkey. Directly above them hovered a very strange cloud, below which another columned cloud perched upon the hill slope. Despite the wind, this cloud never moved. The several hundred soldiers marched on a dangerous offensive into the mists but never emerged from the far side. An hour later the cloud lifted and the men had disappeared with it. In late 1918, after the war, the Turks denied that they had ever captured or engaged these missing troops. It was as if they had been spirited away.

An excellent investigation of historical data was mounted by researcher Paul Begg who checked facts that were widely assumed by other authors to be true. Indeed, the story frequently appeared in mystery books over the next three decades. Begg's research, however, encountered some serious problems.

The First-Fourth was apparently not involved in any vanishing trick, but another group (the First-Fifth) was. This was not a regiment but a battalion, a much smaller body of men.

Historical records, indeed, note that on 12 August (not 21 August as reported), many of these men vanished, though not into a mysterious cloud. Moreover, even their puzzling loss is partially explained. War records show that the group continued to fight, and that after hostilities ended, the bodies of some 122 of the 266 missing men were found. Presumably others were killed in the fighting but their bodies had not been traced three years later.

Frederick Reichardt's son confirmed in 1982, after his father's death, that he had been told the story of the vanishing 'regiment' during the Gallipoli campaign soon after his birth in 1932. Thus it had not suddenly been invented at the fiftieth reunion in 1965, as many sceptics had previously argued. Clearly it was based on some sort of actual episode.

As for the strange cloud, Begg discovered that a very unusual mist and cloud formation was reliably seen to have covered the area on 21 August and that this was noted in the record books on the opposite page to the reference to the disappearance of the First-Fifth soldiers nine days previously.

Begg concluded that the two unrelated events were confused in the minds of Reichardt and his colleagues down the years, particularly given the scars of war they had endured after 1915. A curious misty cloud was indeed seen. A few hundred men did vanish, but not inexplicably so. And the link between the two events that has forged a supernatural legend was merely a coincidence.

Of course, nobody can ever prove, as these eyewitnesses contended to their dying day, that the 144 men still unaccounted for did not vanish in some supernatural fashion. As such the legend will endure.

The *Bowmen of Mons*, by A. Forestier, used in the Christmas edition of the *London Illustrated News*, 1915.

1916 SUMMER

GHOSTLY PHOTOGRAPH

One of the first impressive photographs of an apparition was taken in Tingewick, Buckinghamshire, southern England, by a retired police detective inspector. His picture showed three women enjoying a garden party; but intruding into the image was the figure of a semi-transparent, ghost-like dog. Nobody at the time remembered seeing it appear or depart. Was it a pet back from the grave?

The ghostly dog at the Tingewick tea party.

1917

FAIRIES AT THE BOTTOM OF THE GARDEN

Although few people, even in rural communities, any longer believed in fairies, two young cousins in the suburb of Cottingley, on the outskirts of Bradford, West Yorkshire, England, certainly did. And the evidence they produced was at the heart of a strange case that received wide publicity.

Fourteen-year-old Elsie Wright often played with 10-year-old Frances Griffiths in the wooded beck at the rear of her house.

The famous photograph of the Cottingley gnome, later admitted to have been a hoax.

For both girls it was a magical place, for they had regularly observed fairies – small, ethereal, flying creatures – forming out of thin air in the bushes.

Their stories were not believed. Elsie's father was particularly dismissive, and mainly unhappy that they got dirty or wet in the process, conduct in those days unbecoming of a young lady.

Opinions changed, however, on a day in July when the girls borrowed his camera. Mr Wright developed one photograph on which some strange white blobs showed up. These crystallized into an image of dancing fairies parading in front of Frances, who was gazing not at the weird spirits but straight at the camera. When later asked about this oddity, the girls explained that they saw fairies all of the time but having your photograph taken was a novelty!

A month later Frances filmed Elsie playing with a gnome. The manner in which her hand was outstretched was later ascribed by psychic sources to mystic energies, though Frances matter of factly explained it as the result of her ineptitude behind the lens. The girls showed these pictures to friends and tried to convince Mr Wright, who still thought them fakes. It was only two years later when Mrs Wright, who was interested in the supernatural, took them to a meeting of psychics in Bradford, that the story took off.

31

Psychic researchers, who mounted an investigation, were divided about the authenticity of the two photographs. It was pointed out that the images looked suspiciously two-dimensional and in focus, whereas the background views of the girls themselves were more fuzzy. Moreover, the fairies had surprisingly modern hairstyles. Even noted fairy lore experts found that a bit much to swallow. Nobody examined the original plates and, on the assumption that 'a picture is worth a thousand words', the testimony of the two girls went unchallenged. Little heed was paid to the fact, either, that Elsie had worked for a photog-

Above left and right: two of the 'Cottingley Fairies' photographs.
Left: the banks of the beck at Cottingley, playground of the 'fairies'.

rapher for some months and was quite a talented artist, constantly drawing fairies (because, as she remarked, she was always seeing them).

The girls were reunited in 1920, but although they were lent a new camera, in the presence of others they always failed to produce an image. Left on their own some time later, they did, nevertheless, obtain three more fairy photographs. Finally, in August 1921, a noted psychic was sent to the beck and 'saw' the fairies along with Frances, but no photographs proved possible. After that the girls moved apart and stopped seeing anything strange. But they had left a legacy of five photographs that continued to intrigue believers and doubters alike.

By coincidence Sir Arthur Conan Doyle was writing an article on fairies for the Christmas 1920 edition of *Strand* magazine precisely when this saga began. He used the first two photographs (and the latter three during a 1921 sequel) to press his case that fairies were real. His belief in them partly derived from his father, diagnosed mentally ill, who had long reported seeing them. Doyle also held deep Spiritualist convictions about the existence of other dimensions.

In 1922, Doyle, having largely abandoned his best-selling fictions to focus on psychic research, published his work on elementals, *The Coming of the Fairies*, which legitimized the photographs of Elsie and Frances for all the world to see. Fairies were a popular topic of conversation. More books followed and fairy sightings were collected, a few still being reported even today.

Much later, with the advent of modern technology, the rather dubious nature of the Cottingley photographs soon became evident. Computer enhancement techniques developed from the deep space programme showed the fairies to be two-dimensional and probably mere paper cut-outs. But the two women, still alive fifty years after their adventure, refused to admit that they had been cheating. In 1966 Elsie spoke of filming 'figments of my imagination' and on BBC TV in 1971 just wanted to leave the subject 'open'.

The truth, if truth it be, emerged only a decade later shortly before the cousins died. Both finally confessed that the first four photographs were outright hoaxes. The images were simply paper drawings by Elsie. Indeed they pointed to the fact that

you could see the head of the hat pin that was holding up the gnome. It was sticking out of the figure's chest; although Conan Doyle had thought this to be a psychic umbilical cord!

As for the fifth image, which is somewhat less clear or two-dimensional, a curious discrepancy has emerged. Elsie said that it was also a hoax just like the other four, but Frances until her death was adamant that this was the only real fairy photograph the two girls ever took.

These hoax photographs date from a time when the world was on a threshold between dying beliefs in magic and folklore and emergent scientific supremacy. They offer many telling lessons to supernatural researchers. Later popularization of other strange images suggest that these lessons went largely unheeded even in a much more hi-tech society.

Hoax or not, the Cottingley fairy photographs have one final twist to offer, which may never be resolved. Both Elsie Wright and Frances Griffiths, even on their death beds, insisted that regardless of the status of their much debated photographs there were real fairies and elves in Cottingley beck and that they both often saw them.

1917 MAY – OCTOBER

THE FÁTIMA MIRACLE

On 13 May 1917 two girls and a boy aged between 6 and 9 years old were tending sheep in the rural area of Fátima, in northern Portugal, when a beam of light flashed from the sky and a small, glowing figure of a woman, clothed in a strange radiance, appeared. She spoke of coming from heaven and asked the children to return on the 13th of each successive month. The story soon got out and on the 13th of each month a crowd gathered. Only the original three witnesses ever saw the being. They called it an 'angel'; but the church authori-

ties soon interpreted it as 'the Virgin Mary'.

Prophecies were given: one of the imminent Russian Revolution and the other about World War Two. Neither, however, was publicly revealed until after these events occurred. A third prophecy was given by the children under seal to the Vatican telling of a major trauma still to come.

This third prophecy was reportedly opened in secret by the pope in 1960 but – despite instructions to do so – not then revealed to the world. Rumours as to its content include a nuclear war, natural global disaster and the destruction of the Catholic Church.

The final visit of the 'angel' was on 17 October. A crowd of 70,000-100,000 gathered this time from far and wide to see a predicted 'miracle'. Many onlookers insisted that a hole was punched through a raincloud at noon and a spinning disc, presumably the Sun, poured down great heat and blinding radiance on to the ground, before corkscrewing earthwards and then retreating up again. No attestable photographs of this phenomenon exist despite extensive eyewitness accounts.

Sceptics argue that this was an optical illusion brought on by mass hysteria and intense expectation. A more recent theory has developed that these visits were really by aliens in a UFO masquerading as a religious miracle.

Since the visions at Fátima, the village has become a world-famous centre of pilgrimage.

1919 MAY

LIVING FOSSIL

A miner extracting coal far below the surface of the Netherseal Colliery north-east of Birmingham in the English Midlands found a small brown toad buried alive inside a coal seam. Not resembling any normal toad, it measured only 3 inches in diameter, and appeared to be blind and to have no mouth. But it was undoubtedly alive and adjusted to its surroundings over the next few days.

There are many other reliable instances of small animals being found alive inside lumps of rock. The coal seam would have formed 200 million years ago, so most sceptics assume that the animal somehow entered a crack and became trapped there after its birth in recent times. However, there are those who speculate that the creature might have entered when the rock first formed and then lived in 'suspended animation' for millennia, or that it was teleported through time and space directly into the rock cavity.

In truth, nobody knows how these embedded animals get there.

THE ROARING TWENTIES

This decade, for all its postwar uncertainties, was in many ways an exciting period. Electric lighting and cars were becoming commonplace. The cinema was a popular art form. Radio was entering many homes and 'talking radio' (television) was under development. Science emphasized the way in which invisible rays could travel through space and create action at a distance.

All this affected the world of the paranormal. Science fiction, too, looked to the future with stories of robots and civilization to come, reflecting the spirit of the age. And having conquered the air, thoughts turned to the next great frontier. One day we might have the ability to reach the stars.

1920 1929

1922

THE CURSE OF KING TUTANKHAMUN

The Earl of Carnarvon had spent many years in Egypt with his young protégé and mentor Howard Carter expending vast sums of money in the search for the fabled treasure-laden tomb of the boy king Tutankhamun. By late 1922, on the verge of giving up the quest in despair, he made a discovery that was to turn into one of the most frightening stories of the century.

On 4 November, the sealed tomb was found in the only small area they had not so far searched. The earl was back in England but sailed immediately to the Valley of the Kings near Luxor. On 26 November, with Carter and the crew, he cleared the last pieces of rubble to enter the sacred ruins that had remained untouched for 3000 years. As an early omen, the lucky canary that the team had with them was eaten by a cobra that stole into its cage. This snake was the ancient protective symbol of pharaoh kings. Immediately, dread descended upon the local workers.

After some weeks of wrangles with the Egyptian government over ownership of the bejewelled golden artefacts and other marvels in this long-sought historic treasure, Carnarvon developed a strange malady. At first it was thought to be a fever, then blood poisoning was diagnosed. In early April 1923 he collapsed into a coma at a Cairo hotel. He never recovered.

According to eyewitnesses, including his family and Howard Carter, at the very point of his death the hotel lights flickered and went out. The electricity was off for five minutes in an unexplained power loss. Back in England, apparently at the same moment, the Carnarvons' housekeeper noticed the family terrier let out a terrible howl and collapsed dead on to the carpet.

When these stories were all combined, the notion rapidly took hold that there was a curse associated with the tomb. It was considered that the dead king's spirit had been disturbed and was seeking revenge.

Although the curse theory seems somewhat tenuous, a number of people loosely associated with the opening of the tomb did die at a relatively early age. The nurse who looked after Carnarvon during his fatal illness, for example, died in childbirth when just 28.

View from the Nile of the Valley of the Kings.

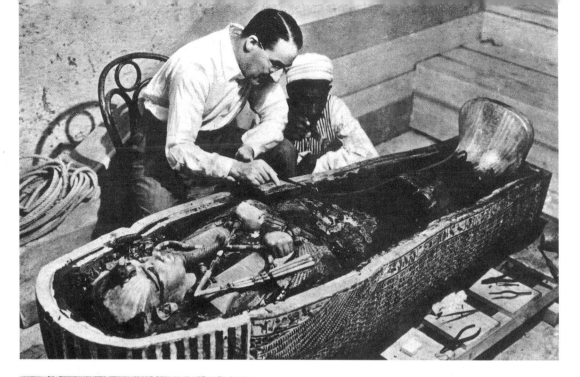

Top: Howard Carter examining the sarcophagus of Tutankhamun. Above: Carter supervising the opening of Tutankhamun's tomb.

As years have gone by, the legend of the curse has remained strong. Claims of a protective force have long attached themselves to the desecration of a pharaoh's remains, and very few people have since appeared to be willing to take any chances by defying the curse.

When the exhibits from the tomb were put on display in London in 1972, the director of antiquities in charge of these arrangements was one of the brave who openly scoffed at the curse, stating that he was fit and healthy at 52 after a lifetime of working with such tomb artefacts. Days later he dropped dead.

1922 8 MARCH

SHOWERS OF STONES

Possibly the best attested case of mystery objects falling out of the sky occurred beside the railway tracks at Chico, California. It lasted seven days and, despite a major police on-site operation, was never explained.

Stones varying in size from small pebbles to large rocks cascaded down on to the roof of a grain warehouse and several surrounding houses. The local fire chief and police officer, investigating the riddle, had a narrow escape when a large boulder crashed out of the sky on to a fence beside them. Charles Fort documented this episode, which ended as suddenly as it began.

Over the years all manner of objects have rained down inexplicably from clear skies.

The list most commonly includes fish, seeds and even coins. Theories range from transportation by whirlwind or tornado (which only make sense in incidents more isolated than that at Chico) to poltergeist attacks by invisible and malicious sprites.

1927 APRIL

FOOTPRINT IN THE CANYON

Prospectors discovered a most unusual fossil in Fisher Canyon, Nevada, USA. Embedded in the rock was what appeared to be the print of a human shoe, unmistakably a piece of manufactured footwear with stitching. The only problem is that the oldest known human being lived some 10-15 million years ago and certainly did not wear shoes. This rock was formed over 160 million years ago – long before it is even remotely conceivable that any human life on Earth existed.

Arguments about this evidence range from sceptics, who suggest it was carved into the rock long ago, but within historical time, possibly by Native Americans, to the idea that it might be proof that extraterrestrials or time travellers visited our planet in the distant geological past.

TRACKING THE BLACK BEAST

Throughout the world, but notably in Britain, there are legendary tales about the 'black dog', a monstrous animal that stalks lonely roadways. It goes by many names, such as 'black shuck', and can be found visibly portrayed in a number of pub signs and names attached to ancient inns.

At Bungay, Suffolk, eastern England, in August 1577, a black dog is alleged to have appeared in the aisle of a packed church during a violent electrical storm and to have burned worshippers with some kind of devilish fire, killing three of them. Burn

Marks allegedly made by the phantom black dog on the door inside Blythburgh church.

marks, which are attributed to that terrible day, still exist on the wooden door of the church. A similar occurrence was reported not far away at the village of Blythburgh.

In other cases, the association with electricity is strongly noted, implying to some that these weather conditions awaken the creature.

In 1927 modern evidence for the black dog mystery took a dramatic turn with an incident on the Isle of Man, where the beast is called the 'Moddey Dhoo'. A man on a country road near Ramsey spotted a black shape looming in front of him. He identified it as a huge dog with coal-red eyes that flashed fiercely (the most consistent feature of these black dog stories). The animal blocked the path of the traveller for some time, then moved aside. Shortly afterwards the man's father died, reinforcing the belief in rural circles that sightings are a bad omen.

The phantom nature of the animal is further attested by the way in which it vanishes suddenly after its task is done. It is also reported to leave behind a sulphurous odour, although in more recent cases this has been likened to an electrical burning or arcing smell. This often led to early beliefs that the dog was Satan in disguise or a guardian of the dead, protecting church-yards.

Paranormal researcher Jerome Clark tells how his father had 'the strangest experi-ence' in the early 1920s at La Crosse, Wis-consin. He saw shining eyes and the face of a dog with a dark looming mass behind it. When he saw it again at the same spot some days later, he kicked out at it, only to find his foot suddenly lodged inside the mouth of the beast, as if it had anticipated his

Right: Jerome Clark, whose father had a frightening experience with a black dog.
Below: Lithograph of a witch riding a black dog.

actions. The young man screamed aloud and the horrible apparition vanished.

However, the fact that these creatures 'haunt' certain locations has provoked more recent ideas that the 'black dog' may be a glowing energy form perhaps created within the atmosphere at particular places and existing only for a brief period, not unlike ball lightning. Its 'devilish' odour may result from gases in the atmosphere being electrolysed by the thing's energy output. The identification of the form as a black dog may owe more to legend and tra-dition creating patterns of expectation that a witness 'reads into' the glowing amor-phous mass than is actually present.

If this is true, it would explain why black dog sightings are less common today, although they do still occasionally happen. Perhaps the glowing mass is now being evaluated by witnesses in a new way, e.g. as a UFO.

Intriguingly, there are cases that might support such a view. UFO entities have been reported, for example, with glowing red eyes. Leiston churchyard in Suffolk has also had several black dog sightings throughout the centuries. Yet in February 1975 a real dog and its owner on the beach here observed a glowing pear-shaped mass that floated across the sand toward them. The dog fled in terror while its master suffered physical ill effects (e.g. nausea), which might suggest that a radiating energy field was being emitted by the thing. A pungent odour of electrolysed air and nitrogen was left behind.

There is even a classic case of alien space-napping at Todmorden, West Yorkshire, in November 1980 when a policeman related under hypnosis how he had encountered a spinning mass, which had burned the road surface dry and 'stolen' fifteen minutes of his life. On board the spacecraft he had met not only the customary strange alien creatures but also a fierce black dog!

1928 OCTOBER

OZ FACTOR

A young seaman was working aboard an oil tanker on a run from the USA to Europe, a voyage scheduled to last two weeks. The ship was then positioned just east of the Florida mainland.

At 8 p.m. one evening the sailor was in his cabin preparing to visit the library. But a strange calmness had descended upon the vessel. He walked out on to the deck and instinctively knew that something was wrong. To his astonishment, the ship was utterly deserted.

The eerie silence, calmness and isolation that he sensed around him was, as he explained, like being placed inside a ship 'within a glass bottle'. He felt suddenly cut off from the real world. This sensation has become recognized as typical of various paranormal experiences, from apparitions to timeslips and psychic visions to UFO close encounters. It is commonly described as 'all environmental sounds disappearing',

'time standing still' and 'a weird, silvery silence that descends upon the scene'.

The experience has also been defined by the term 'Oz Factor', because the cases in which it occurs cross boundaries between many different phenomena but have one thing in common. The witness appears temporarily to leave the real world and enter a strange one, like the mythical land of Oz, where the normal laws of nature are briefly suspended and magical things can happen.

The seaman wandered along the flat surface of the vessel, searching everywhere for somebody and surveying the odd way in which sky and sea had blended into one seamless whole, monotone grey in colour. As he walked the several hundred yards of deck, he met nobody. The dozens of crewmen had disappeared. Nothing changed in the skies about him and he sat on a narrow deckway, head in hands, in despair.

Then, suddenly, he heard running footsteps. He looked up and saw a shipmate asking where he had been. On his failure to arrive in the library, they had started to look for him, but although they scoured the ship, he had completely vanished for some time. The walkway was too narrow to allow two people to pass without notice. They had been extremely worried, fearing he might have fallen overboard.

Gazing up at the sky, the man could see that all was normal once again. The oppressiveness of a leaden atmosphere and time suspension had disappeared. He was back from Oz.

1928 II OCTOBER

SIGNALS FROM SPACE

During the 1920s there were persistent reports that experiments with new radio transmitting equipment were producing unexpected sounds. Their source appeared to be somewhere in outer space.

In fact, Nikola Tesla, working in the USA, had reportedly first detected ordered echoes on his equipment as far back as 1899, but few had taken the rather eccentric and mystically minded inventor too seriously at the time.

In August 1921 Guglielmo Marconi, doing experiments to develop the use of radio for Morse-coded message communication, picked up regular signals from space that he interpreted as being a coded sequence. He suggested (some thought sarcastically) that they might come from Martians!

Exactly three years later, astronomers revived this 'wild' story when Mars came very near Earth in its orbital path. As radio stations were then very few in number, but rapidly on the increase, they knew that this might be the last chance to scan the planet at such close range for any intelligently originated signals before the strength of radio traffic swamped any weak space messages. Using a new technique that turned electrical signals, like radio, into a photographic image, they tuned into the red planet. The results proved amazing – a sequence of dots and dashes that bore a vague resemblance to a human face was received.

In 1927 American radio engineers attempted to locate the actual source of all these messages and found that they seemed to emerge from just a few thousand miles out from the Earth's surface.

The following year, at the Philips radio factory in Eindhoven, Holland, Jorgen Hals (his findings later confirmed by Professor Carl Stormer, a radio expert in Oslo, Norway) detected consistently delayed 'echoes', each lasting about three seconds, that were appearing in their respective transmissions. Whereas they knew by now that radio transmissions could bounce off the ionosphere (a layer of charged particles in the upper atmosphere), the latter was so close to Earth that the echo could not possibly last three seconds. For an echo of that duration, the sounds had to be bouncing back from beyond the orbit of the Moon.

This implied that the signal was being sent back from something floating freely in outer space.

The most important message was first received on 11 October 1928 when the echo was suddenly no longer of regular duration. It began to vary between three and fifteen seconds. It was always on the same wavelength (31.4 metres). A team at King's College, London, heard the mystery message on 19 February 1929 and it was received for the last time in France three months later.

The enigma was never solved, although later theories suggested that the radio waves slowed down as they passed through charged particle layers close to the ionosphere. After the messages ceased in 1929, the radio scientists gave up and all was forgotten for nearly twenty years. By 1947, when new attempts were made to tune in with better equipment, interference from Earth stations was so intense that it proved impossible.

In an article for the magazine *Spaceflight* in 1973, science writer and Scottish astronomer Duncan Lunan plotted the 1920s signals as if they were meant to represent data from a star map. From this he reached the astonishing conclusion that they could be a picture of the Epsilon Bootis system. He went on to suggest that the message was from an artificial probe sent to our solar system from a planet around that distant star and left to wait until radio transmissions from Earth swept outward through space, thus indicating that our technology had reached a sufficiently advanced level. Then it would start releasing a pulsed echo on a pre-arranged cue by reflecting these signals back and providing the star map that proved its intelligent origin.

Unfortunately, the data did not exactly coincide with the star system, and there were so few points on the map (only half a dozen, in fact) that it might simply appear to fit by chance. Furthermore, in order to match up these stellar positions of the Epsilon Bootis system, Lunan had to assume that the probe had been sent 13,000 years ago.

Of course, it was not unreasonable that such an unmanned probe might have been sent all that time back, lying dormant in a 'parking' orbit beyond the Moon waiting for the Earth to develop radio technology. Lunan admitted that he offered the idea more as a scientific exercise than statement of certainty, and it never became widely accepted. But no other explanation has been given for the source of the consistent radio echoes heard between 1927 and 1929.

Perhaps Lunan was right after all in suggesting that the probe switched itself off in 1929 after two fruitless years of trying to attract our attention. It might have sent a message back to Epsilon Bootis to await further instructions or, indeed, to suggest to the message senders that they come to our stellar backwater and take a look for themselves.

If so, then some time in the late twenty-first century we might have some unexpected visitors from a very long way away.

Nikola Tesla, inventor of electrical devices and equipment, picked up some of the earliest signals from space.

A SHRINKING WORLD

Tension mounted gradually throughout the 1930s until the outbreak of World War Two. Yet by now, as air travel became commercialized, the world had shrunk rapidly as journeys that had taken weeks or months were now done in days.

Alongside this literal widening of horizons came a perception of other ways of moving beyond the here and now. Freud and Jung helped to reveal the nature of dreams—mental voyages of incalculable speed and scope. This opened the way to an understanding of mind and consciousness, and the first investigations into extra-sensory perception.

Materialism, the belief structure accepted by most scientists, continued to survive but was threatened by inescapable discoveries about the essence of the Universe.

1930

1930

MYSTERIES OF THE AIR

During the 1920s, several pioneer aviators were involved in tragic disappearances. Sadly, that was to be expected, given that they were flying flimsy aircraft on dangerous treks over deep oceans, and of such duration that they were almost certain to hit bad weather at some point. The wonder is that so many made successful flights to open up the world's airways to relatively safe travel for the masses.

One such disappearance occurred in March 1928 when a hero from World War One, Captain W. Hinchcliffe, left England on an attempt to fly the Atlantic with his female passenger. They vanished without trace. However, eighteen days later a medium named Bea Earl received a message from the pilot, desperately seeking to contact his wife. This was arranged through Sir Arthur Conan Doyle.

Earl, and later the more famous medium Eileen Garrett, established a regular link between Mr and Mrs Hinchcliffe across the spiritual divide. He appeared to be very worried about the prospects for the R101, a gigantic hydrogen-filled airship being developed at Cardington in Bedfordshire. This was a prototype for a fleet of floating passenger vessels designed to carry the wealthy at speed to destinations at the four corners of the world.

Serious problems were already dogging the programme. Yet on 4 October 1930, despite the repeated warnings of Hinchcliffe's spirit that the dirigible could not possibly survive, as well as a vision received by the medium of an airship in flames, the R101 left on a maiden flight to India with forty-eight people on board. Hours later, as it crossed the Channel, Hinchcliffe announced through Mrs Garrett that 'nothing but a miracle can save them'.

The burned-out fuselage of the R101 airship after crashing near Beauvais.

At 2 a.m. on 5 October, flying dangerously low, the airship plunged into a hilly bank near Beauvais in northern France. Within seconds its lighter than air hydrogen gas bags exploded into a massive inferno, giving most on board no possible chance of survival.

The mystery was how the disaster had occurred. Sadly, all the senior crew members and every passenger died in the flames. The six crew survivors were well outside the control room area when the end came.

On 7 October Eileen Garrett took part in a seance organized by researcher Harry Price to try to contact the spirit of the recently deceased Sir Arthur Conan Doyle, who had vowed to prove life after death. But it was not he who spoke through Mrs Garrett that day. It was Flight Lieutenant Irwin, captain of the doomed airship, who insistently hogged the proceedings to offer a comprehensive account as to why the R101 had struck disaster.

Irwin gave many specific details of the problems supposedly involved and spoke of almost hitting rooftops at Achy just before the fatal crash. This place name did not appear in any ordinary atlas but was traced on a very detailed map such as the airship crew would have used for navigation. It was a tiny village near the point where the craft had come down.

Irwin and several other crew members came forward in later seances in an attempt to provide evidence for the accident enquiry. But these statements 'from beyond the grave' contradicted the guesswork of the enquiry members and were excluded from the records. Airship commentators disagreed on the probable authenticity of the detailed seance quotes. One in particular was adamant that the source – strange as it was – could not be the dead captain, since it contained serious errors of fact that the latter would never have made. Many experts accepted that Eileen Garrett's powers were genuine, but telepathic in nature, i.e. capable of reading the minds of those present in the room, rather than making contact with the spirits of the dead crew members. Others still regard the R101 seances as some of the best evidence yet for survival of bodily death.

Throughout the first half of the decade there were also repeated sightings of mysterious aircraft, especially over northern Europe. Between 1932 and 1934 several dozen reports were received from Sweden, Norway and Finland of extreme low-level aircraft with powerful searchlight beams taking to the air in terrible weather conditions, such as fog and blizzards. Military aircraft that were despatched by the baffled authorities were unable to pursue them.

Anders Liljegren gained access to the still-secret files forty years later and found that radio interception of the mysterious contour-hugging planes had been attempted and had failed. Nobody knew what they were and they stopped flying as suddenly as they arrived. They were remarkably like the unidentified airships spotted between 1896 and 1915 and, of course, the UFOs of today.

1933

NESSIE RISES TO THE SURFACE

Loch Ness is a brooding ribbon lake, deep and dark, formed within a geological fault zone west of Inverness in northern Scotland. Its scenic beauty was opened up by a new road built in the late 1920s and this was to have a profound effect upon tourism in this lovely area.

For hundreds of years, in fact, there had been persistent sporadic reports by local villagers of a grey-brown humped creature seen rising to the surface of the loch and rapidly submerging again. Now that the new road allowed an uncluttered view for several miles, passing tourists also had the opportunity to see something strange.

Between 1930 and 1933, there were many sightings that received some local publicity and culminated in the first of many books about the Loch Ness monster, written by Rupert Gould in 1934.

Early reports were merely of unusual wakes and strange wavelike humps. It was the incident on 14 April 1933 that really provoked national, then international, attention. A couple in a car near Abriachan had stopped to observe a large, unknown animal rolling around in the water for several minutes before sinking down. They were in no doubt that what they had seen – and the term was now used for the first time – was indeed the monster.

In the immediate wake of this sighting there were more reports, including several of a lumbering beast said to have crossed the road and crashed through trees into the water. Accounts of Nessie walking on land, however, were intermittent and have since become rarer still.

Then, on 13 November 1933, the first well-considered photograph of the creature was taken by Hugh Gray, a resident of Foyers. It shows a blurred sinewy shape, a bit like a snake, swimming sideways through water. Many sources have since noticed something very odd about this image. Closer viewing suggests an out-of-focus image of a dog with a stick in its mouth swimming straight at the camera; and although this may be sheer coincidence, it is almost impossible thereafter to recapture the initial impression of a snake-like monster. Be that as it may, the photograph offers poor scientific evidence.

Soon afterwards a much more impressive photograph was obtained of Nessie in what has now become its best known form – a long neck popping out of the water, looking rather like that of the aquatic dinosaur *Plesiosaurus*, which many allege it to be. This photograph, usually called the 'surgeon's picture', was soon published by the *Daily Mail*, after which it became famous the world over.

Robert Wilson's famous photograph of the Loch Ness monster has been challenged by the sceptics.

The picture was taken on 19 April 1934 by Robert Wilson, a gynaecologist, who was on shore with several companions when the monster's neck paraded past for a few minutes. Controversy has always surrounded this image. Recent studies by sceptics have argued quite convincingly from the ripple patterns on the water and other factors that the object must be fairly modest in size – probably only a foot or two in length. Therefore it cannot be, as most people, including the photographer, have concluded, the neck of a 20- or 30-foot-long beast some distance from shore.

Then, in 1992, 86-year-old Lambert Wilson (unrelated to the surgeon) came forward to claim that he knew the source of this most celebrated of Nessie photographs. That source was none other than himself!

In fact, he had borrowed a model serpent's head from a store and swum under water, holding it so that it protruded from the surface, at one point being hit by stones thrown by a spectator on shore. Wilson says that he then waited until he could see through eyeholes that someone had taken his picture. He had no idea that his little jest would create such a worldwide furore and appear in countless books and magazines down through the years.

Of course, once set in motion, the Nessie bandwagon was unstoppable. However, although with hindsight much of the early evidence now seems dubious, and although the tourist industry predictably seized upon the friendly 'beastie' as a source of income, the fact remains that persistent stories existed long before this and that much new 'evidence' has since added to the mystery.

Indeed, Loch Ness is by no means the only lake to harbour reports of a monster. Virtually all similar-sized bodies of water in the northern hemisphere (especially in Canada and Scandinavia) carry associated and almost identical legends. In fact, several other lakes in Scotland (notably Loch Morar) and Ireland, have data bases of widespread sightings. The Morar beast (Morag) is considered by some to deserve stronger support than its more celebrated cousin further north.

1934

EXTRA-SENSORY PERCEPTION

ESP has existed as far back as the earliest human societies. In ancient tribal cultures from the African plains to the Australian bush, shamans, or medicine men, occupied a position of honour because of their ability to invoke special powers or display uncanny awareness of things beyond normal experience. They could move the tribe to a location where food or water might be found. They could foresee natural disasters and seek safer ground.

This was long assumed to be one of those human skills beyond understanding, like the homing instinct of birds. It was not systematically studied until the late 1920s, when Dr Joseph Rhine and his wife Louisa obtained grant funding to develop laboratory research under the auspices of the psychology department of Duke University in North Carolina. It was a highly controversial project, sanctioned only by reason of

their scientific and academic background.

By 1934 the Rhines had developed a methodology and technique to apply to endlessly repetitive experiments with subjects who appeared to be what we would now call 'psychic'. Since they were being tested to judge whether they could detect information by means that did not involve the five ordinary senses, the phrase 'extra-sensory perception' was coined to describe what was being contemplated.

The Rhines' team used a simple prop to assist their enquiries – a pack of 25 cards, each carrying one of five distinctive symbols. Thus there were five cards each of a cross, star, square, circle and series of wavy lines. They were called 'Zener cards' after the research aide who worked with them.

The test was simple. The 'sender' picked out one card from the shuffled pack. Elsewhere in the building, the psychic who was being tested attempted to 'guess' which symbol was on that card. As there was a one in five chance of being correct, the odds for success were easily computable. With a trial run of 100 cards, anything above 20 correct guesses would be in excess of what the statistics proposed. Such a result would imply that the 'receiver' was using some sort of perception beyond the capability of the normal senses in order to detect the correct information.

Dr Rhine published the results in 1934, which provoked immediate debate. The figures established the first meaningful data to show that ESP really was possible. Some subjects were able regularly to produce guesses above the 20 per cent mark, although, oddly, they often failed to score much higher. Receivers did not consistently score 20 out of 25, for example, but usually 6 or 7 instead of the expected 5.

Equally, there were other strange problems. It was realized that ESP could operate in several ways. The sender viewing the correct Zener card might transmit that image to the receiver, in which case telepathy was at work; or the receiver might

simply see ahead in time to the point when he would actually know the outcome of the various card runs, in which case the most probable cause was precognition. Alternatively, there might be a process whereby information itself could in some way be accessed directly by the mind, rather like reading the figures off a dial. This form of 'seeing clear' was known by the French term *clairvoyance*.

Dr Rhine's experiments left uncertainties because equally good scores resulted when the receiver never knew how the cards turned out (eliminating the most obvious source of precognition) or when he was asked to predict the run of cards well before these were shuffled and turned over (in which case precognition was the only realistic option).

Most scientists, while impressed by Rhine's approach, were unconvinced by the possibility of unseen and unexplained

Left and below: participants in a corroboree. The paranormal finds ready acceptance in Aboriginal culture.

A SHRINKING WORLD

powers of the mind. So they suggested, particularly with reference to the growing awareness of the statistical nature of subatomic matter, that the reported average scores might result not from ESP but from a misunderstanding of the workings of statistics. In 1937, however, a team of statistical mathematicians checked Rhine's work thoroughly and could find no fault. He was truly getting success above the level dictated by chance. There was no way around that fact.

Yet there were other objections to the Zener card tests. For a start, they were not truly random unless the pack was reshuffled after each one was turned up. This was because, if the receiver guessed correctly that the first card was, say, a circle, then only four circles remained to be turned up in the pack, so that this symbol was obviously statistically less likely to be the next one to appear than the wavy lines or the cross. As the test proceeded, such complex factors came more and more into play.

Despite such drawbacks, this work was a crucial first step toward scientific evaluation of ESP, which continues today in a far more sophisticated manner.

1934 APRIL

LUMINOUS WOMAN

Anna Manaro, a young woman from the village of Pirano, Italy, had just emerged from a religious fast when she developed an extraordinary medical condition which remains inexplicable. Whenever she fell into a deep sleep her body began to glow a vivid electric blue colour from the area around her breasts.

Her condition aroused great interest. On 11 April, Dr Protti from Padua University and a team of five other medical specialists kept a vigil at her bedside and witnessed the amazing phenomenon first hand, taking measurements and some cine film.

Their work demonstrated that the subject doubled her heartbeat and respiratory rate during these brief minutes when the strange glow shone through her skin as if from inside the body. Yet, despite various theories being proposed about 'radiant blood', no solution was ever found. Anna suffered no obvious ill effects from her mysterious affliction and it simply stopped happening in early May after only a few weeks.

1935 JUNE

GLIMPSE OF THE FUTURE

Air Chief Marshal Sir Victor Goddard was an impressive man. As a war hero he led a charmed life. In later years he became one of the first eminent individuals to make a positive statement about the reality of UFOs. In January 1946, he met someone by chance at a cocktail party who predicted he would shortly die. A few hours later he took off on a flight, his plane crashed and he survived. That remarkable, complex tale of precognition was filmed in 1955 as a suspenseful movie, *The Night My Number Came Up*.

However, even more astonishing was Goddard's much earlier encounter with the unknown. This became recognized as vital to our understanding of the nature of time.

On a wet and dismal summer day in 1935, he was flying a Hawker Hart biplane bomber near Edinburgh, Scotland. The cockpit was open and thus he was undoubtedly wide awake. Suddenly, he lost control and plummeted toward the ground, pulling out of the dive at the last minute. Disorientated, he searched for Drem, an old airfield disused for almost twenty years, to serve as a local landmark. He found it, but not as expected.

All at once it was a bright, sunny day and below him was Drem, resplendent, fully operational and modernized. Strange yellow aircraft were on the ground, being supervised by workmen in unrecognizable blue coveralls. Although Goddard swept low above their heads, they appeared not to have heard or seen him. Then, just as abruptly, the scene vanished and he was once more flying in rain-sodden skies.

It was several years before this experience made any sense. For in 1938 Drem was reopened and updated to serve as a flight training school. With the approach of war, a fleet of new trainer aircraft was moved in, painted yellow as all future training craft would be, and tended by mechanics in strange blue uniforms.

Somehow this experienced pilot had slipped three or four years into the future.

1939 27 FEBRUARY

THE BORLEY RECTORY HAUNTING

In the 1930s there was little competition for the title of the most haunted house in the world. It was Borley Rectory, on the Essex/Suffolk border in eastern England.

The rectory had been built in 1863 on the site of an older building and, reportedly, of an even earlier abbey. Few people liked the atmosphere of the house and some residents stayed a very short time. They reported seeing ghostly figures, a phantom horse and coaches, and other glowing shapes. Objects would move about on their own, the doorbell would ring incessantly when nobody was present, footsteps would echo across the floor and lights would switch themselves on and off.

After a new vicar moved into the premises in 1929, the haunting turned into a vicious and unrelenting series of poltergeist attacks, in which bottles were thrown and showers of stones pelted against the walls. Noted ghost-hunter Harry Price became involved and spent much time investigating the apparitions. It was his intervention that fostered the property's eerie reputation, even though some criticized him for his gullible or (with less justi-

The charred ruins of Borley Rectory, 1939.

fication) fraudulent work at the site.

A photograph of a brick is a case in point. Price said it was hovering in mid-air due to some unseen force. Sceptics suggested that it might simply have been frozen conveniently *in situ* by the camera.

Following further apparitions and violent assaults by a poltergeist which seemed intent on throwing almost anything it could lay its hand on, a seance was held and a dire warning issued that the house would be burned to the ground. The fire would start above the hall, and buried beneath the wrecked building would be the remains of a long-dead girl whose restless spirit was the source of much of the activity.

The predicted date for the disaster was the night of 27 March 1938. Unsurprisingly, nothing happened.

Yet exactly eleven months later, on 27 February 1939, Borley Rectory did come to a fiery end. The mysterious fire began above the hall, and deep underneath the ruined building were indeed discovered the ancient skeletal remains of a young woman, exactly as predicted.

Although Borley Rectory is no more, the ruined grounds are still visited by people and have continued to generate reports of strange sounds and the occasional apparition. It seems that even the dreadful fire failed to quell completely the restless spirits of this most haunted place.

51

DISCOVERY AND DISASTER

It is said that there is no better spur to human progress than warfare. That was certainly true of the profound changes that emerged from this horror-filled decade.

Major breakthroughs in science, geared toward winning the war, were conducted in top secrecy, culminating in the terrible reality of the first atomic bomb, and fostering rumours of even more devastating experiments. In the postwar world this cover-up mentality persisted as strange lights appeared in the skies and other paranormal phenomena were recorded. As the first unwieldy computers were manufactured in the initial development of artificial intelligence, science persisted in regarding mankind as a super-computer. The new war between science and the supernatural was about to erupt.

1940  1949

1940

PHOTOGRAPHING GHOSTS

Progress in photography was partly fuelled by the wartime need for millions of aerial reconnaissance shots of enemy territory. This sparked increasing interest in the ability to photograph the unseen world of the paranormal, particularly that of spectral apparitions.

The quest received impetus from cases where an image turned up on film without any deliberation on the part of the photographer. In southern England, at St Nicholas Church in Arundel, Sussex, in 1940, a local lawyer who was filming the interior discovered a floating white mass when the picture was developed. It certainly resembles a ghostly priest kneeling by the altar, although the witness insists that nobody was present during the few moments needed to take the photograph.

There were plenty of other cases just like this.

The sceptics' movement argued that accidental fogging of film occasionally produced a ghostlike effect upon development. Sometimes, if the shutter was left open for several seconds to account for the low light levels in a church, for example, someone could walk past the lens and not appear properly exposed because of this short duration. An ethereal effect might result. The doubters were quick to produce hoax pictures to show how easy it was.

The use of infra-red film which operates within the part of the spectrum beyond the visible was perceived as a way of picking up things that the eye could not detect. Some strange blobs were produced by this means, but nothing that resembled a recognizable phantom.

Taking photographs at seances, where mediums deliberately attempted to evoke the spirits of the dead for purposes of communication, had already become popular. Infra-red was useful here because most seances took place in absolute darkness and normal photography was almost impossible.

The kneeling monk photographed in Arundel Church.

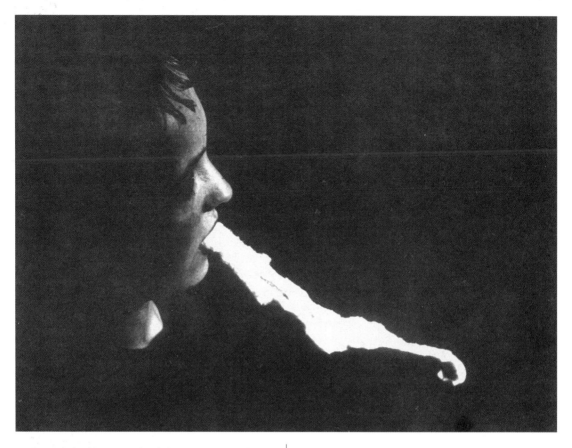

Certainly, hoaxes had been exposed in this fashion. Ghosts that looked very mysterious under the combined effects of the blackout and the heavy aura of expectation surrounding the sitters seemed decidedly more human on secretly processed film. Trumpets raised into the air by spectral forces evidently had a little help on the way from hands of flesh and blood.

Nevertheless, some images that emerged from seances did look very interesting. Ectoplasm – a strange, white doughlike substance said to extrude from the navel, mouth or nose of certain mediums – was filmed more than once. It was said to be used by the spirits as a kind of plasticine for moulding a temporary physical presence on Earth. Although the sceptics charged fraud, alleging it to be probably some sort of thin cloth that had been stuffed into the mouth or down the medium's clothing

Above and right: experiments with mediums producing ectoplasm have always aroused controversy.

before the seance, some seemingly well-attested cases did survive their challenge.

The availability of ever improving photographic techniques deterred the guilty from cooperating fully in these tests and effectively weeded out many of the tricksters who were reluctant to allow the camera in. Yet those who were sincere were happy to support further experiments since they were as eager as anyone else to provide hard evidence that life after death was not merely possible but even certain.

Although science might scoff, ordinary people, particularly those who had lost loved ones during the war, refused to agree. The motivation to believe in the survival of the soul after death was almost irresistible.

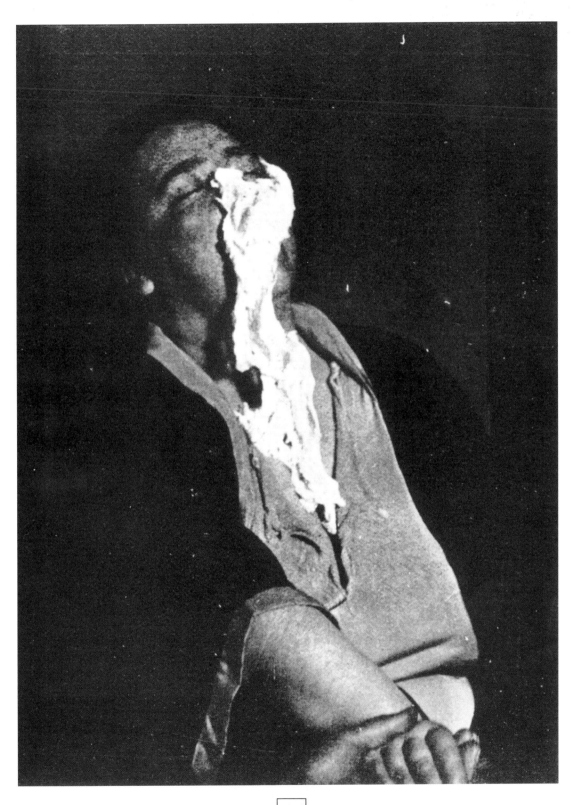

1942

SPACENAPPING

In 1942 the war was reaching its climax. The tide was turning in favour of the Allies but the end was still a very long way off for most suffering people.

This year was apparently the starting point for a mystery that was to become increasingly complex and hotly debated as the century progressed: the abduction of people on both sides of the Atlantic by alien entities.

Although no actual cases were reported at the time – presumably because of other major distractions and possibly memory blocks – and despite the fact that flying saucers, UFOs and alien contact were still unknown, later research revealed an intriguing correlation.

The American cases were brought to light by Budd Hopkins, a New York artist, who since the mid-1970s has been working with people reporting periods of time oddly missing from their lives. He discovered that these strange blackouts could be relieved under regression hypnosis. In some cases the gap was filled by the forgotten memory of a traumatic alien contact. Moreover, this seemed to be an ongoing process that had begun in childhood.

The pattern of contact that tends to begin as far back as the cradle has since been established throughout the world. Hopkins now works with children at as young an age as possible in order to pinpoint an abductee at the onset of what he believes is a lifelong monitor operation somehow set in motion by alien intelligences.

Hopkins found that many of his original contact subjects had been born in 1942/3. It was as if an alien study programme had been initiated at that time. A Canadian lawyer told how as a very young child, when staying at a farm near Lake Superior, Manitoba, she and her family had a conscious memory of finding a calf with a strange, painless, bloody cut on its body. Under hypnosis she 'recalled' having had blood taken from her own leg and making contact with little creatures who told her about life in the Universe and their need to study her.

Another incident occurred in June 1942, when a teenaged boy and girl climbed a hill in the Pennines, in northern England, to look for spent bullets from an army practice range. Suddenly, a strange calm descended on them and they entered the Oz Factor state where the world changed in the blink of an eye. They felt very tired and sat on the grass, only to be interrupted from this summer reverie by two men, one of whom held a curious implement.

These handsome figures seemed godlike rather than merely human, and enveloped in a shimmering haze. They stood over the children discussing them intently, commenting on the nature of time and implying strongly that they would all meet again in the future. When the youngsters asked who the strangers were, one of them looked skyward and remarked wistfully: 'I come from a long way away.' There was then a jump in memory, which has never been recalled, and the children regained full awareness to find the strangers had gone.

Making their way down from the hill, they were greeted by worried relatives and friends. The youngsters had assumed that they were missing for just a couple of hours. In fact it had been a full day and night. Both had puncture wounds and slight bruises on their arms at the point where the brachial artery was located. They had no idea how they had obtained these.

Hypnosis was not applied in their case, so we may never know if there is more background information that has been blocked from recall.

The first consciously remembered spacenapping incident occurred three months

UFO lights sighted above the Capitol in Washington DC proved to be reflections from street lamps.

later. Albert Lancashire was then a young soldier guarding a sentry box on the perimeter of a top-secret radar station near Newbiggin on the Northumberland coast of England.

He observed a weird 'black cloud', with a light in the centre, roll in off the sea. When he went to investigate the curiosity, he was felled by an emergent yellow beam of light. He was left with a floating sensation and then found himself wandering about in a daze for an unknown period of time. He felt that more had occurred and that he had been inside a strange room, but did not recall any details.

In 1967, a full twenty-five years later, Albert saw a series of strange lights shining from the signal box on a railway line in Ashton-under-Lyne, Lancashire, where he was then working. An alien figure also appeared in his bedroom one night. This opened the floodgates and he remembered more fully what had happened in 1942 after the beam of light had struck.

Albert said he had been carried into a room by small creatures and medically examined on a long table in the presence of a taller, more human-like man. He was forced to wear some 'goggles' over his eyes. A woman with 'oriental' features, such as slanted eyes and pasty skin, was also involved. He knew there was more to it than this and sensed that there was a message of spiritual importance from religious beings. But without hypnosis, which has again not been applied, this is as much as we know.

1943

PROJECT INVISIBILITY

One of the most bizarre and yet persistent stories of the second half of the century is the claim that a series of top-secret and devastating experiments was conducted by the US Navy during World War Two. The pro-gramme went by the name of the Philadelphia Experiment, since it was said to have occurred in the breakwater outside this naval dockyard.

The legend first surfaced in January 1956 in two letters sent to a relatively restrained writer on UFOs, Morris Jessup, following publication of his 1955 book *The Case for the UFO*, in which he appealed for research into Einstein's much vaunted unified field theory. The letters, sent by a man calling himself Carlos Allende (then, later, just Carl Allen) were rambling and badly written, with peculiar spelling and punctuation, and of such a nature that Jessup appears to have paid them only slight attention. Indeed, the writer was scathing about Jessup's book and its modest call for more research into energy fields.

Allen claimed that he had been serving on a US ship in 1943 and had witnessed an experiment that made a destroyer completely invisible. He offered quite a lot of detail about this and argued that because of the terrible consequences to the men aboard the ship (including some who went mad, some who burned to a crisp and others who simply vanished) any resumption of such research should be prevented.

This improbable tale nevertheless took a wild turn some months later when Jessup was invited to Washington DC by the Office of Naval Research (ONR). He was met by two senior officers, one of them Commander George Hoover, who was in charge of special projects for the navy. Their involvement gave credibility to the legend.

Hoover showed Jessup a copy of his own book which had been sent to the ONR complete with pages of annotations, apparently a three-way conversation between unknown people who dropped asides such as 'if only he knew'. Jessup identified Carl Allen's handwriting as the individual simply named 'A'. The others were 'B' and 'Jemi'. The notes covered various subjects, including the experiment. The ONR had received these shortly before Allen wrote to Jessup.

Rather more impressed by overt government interest, Jessup handed copies of the letters from Allen to the ONR, who paid for a limited edition of all this material, including Jessup's book and the weird annotations. It was printed by the Varo publishing company (which handled government contracts) and was sent out to various naval sources for comment.

Not surprisingly, this strange sequence of events fuelled speculation as to the possible truth of the otherwise absurd story from the elusive and untraced Carl Allen. Yet the ONR have always insisted that no government money went into this work. It was a private interest by two naval officers who funded it themselves.

Nevertheless, Jessup handed over his material to a friend, admitting that he was 'afraid'. Soon afterwards, in April 1959, he was found dead in his car, having apparently committed suicide.

A man claiming to be Allen came forward ten years later to tell a UFO group that he had hoaxed the entire story (except, of course, the ONR interest in it). He later recanted the confession and that still appears to be his position. However, his family have described him to enquiring researchers as a drifter and a liar; and other evidence implies that he has a rather fertile imagination. Few people now accept his story.

In 1978 a novel entitled *Thin Air*, by George Simpson and Neal Burger (who also wrote an excellent dramatization of the Manhattan Project), reported on the same experiments in fictionalized form. And in 1979 Charles Berlitz and William Moore published a factual investigation, after tracking down Allen and obtaining more data from him (e.g. that the ship supposedly used in the tests was the USS *Eldridge*). They established only a limited amount of hard evidence that something might have happened.

A movie, officially said to be based on the Berlitz/Moore non-fiction, but actually

Morris Jessup was involved in the extraordinary case of the Philadelphia Experiment in which a destroyer was allegedly made to vanish.

mere speculation, appeared in 1984. One viewer of this was Al Bielek, who in September 1989 came forward to allege that it had awoken his memory of being one of the sailors lost aboard the *Eldridge* in 1943!

The full story, based on the combined evidence of the various sources, is that Tesla, Einstein and others began work in the late 1930s to find protection against newly discovered radar waves. By manipulating energy fields they got more than they bargained for and created optical invisibility. Despite reservations by the scientists themselves, wartime pressure forced a 'live' test on the ship, complete with crew, and several runs occurred between July and September 1943 (Allen claimed October). On one test the ship became invisible but left an impression in the water. In another

DISCOVERY AND DISASTER

it was transported through space and later returned to Philadelphia. Bielek alleges that he and another man jumped ship mid-experiment as the sailors aboard had not been warned of the risks they faced. They landed in a naval dockyard forty years into the future (1983) – where scientists from 'Project Rainbow' were expecting them!

Established as true is that the USS *Eldridge* was a real ship, was in the area at the time (being officially 'commissioned' in July 1943) and that Allen really did serve on the ship that he named in his 1956 letters, together with other people whom he also named. Researcher Paul Begg, while properly sceptical of this story, found documents that confirmed Allen's service record. He concluded, however, that there was no way that Allen's ship could have passed close enough to the *Eldridge* to witness such an experiment in October 1943, although it would have been just about possible in July/August 1943 – the dates that Bielek has since claimed.

What is certainly true is that even if Allen's book annotations were only speculations, they were very advanced for 1955. He described two types of alien as being in contact with Earth – LM (large men?), who were basically friendly, and SM (small men?), rather less so. We now know that this is how alien contact evidence is reported. Allen also spoke of objects and people being teleported via these force fields through space and time, and that when such processes are in operation, 'a foggy green mist' forms around the transported object. There are several impressive eyewitness accounts of this phenomenon later than 1955. It is unlikely that the participants have ever heard of Carl Allen and yet they describe being moved through space and time by a mist (often green) which generates an intense electrical field around it.

Indeed, historical records even show that back in July/August 1904 – thirty-nine years to the week before the alleged experiments

began – curious and violent electrical fields struck the area around Philadelphia a devastating blow. One ship (the *Mohican*) was even surrounded by a glowing electrified cloud which caused the sailors' beards to jut out and magnetized all metal aboard.

1945 5 DECEMBER

THE DISAPPEARANCE OF FLIGHT 19

On this day six military aircraft vanished within a few hours of one another, sparking off one of the greatest of all aviation mysteries. The legend that it created remains intact today but seems to rest on far shakier foundations than is appreciated.

Flight 19 comprised five Grumman TBM Avenger bombers containing fourteen men, all inexperienced students except for their trainer, Lieutenant Charles Taylor. He was a practised flier but had just moved to Fort Lauderdale, Florida, from Miami and had not flown this training route before.

The mission left at 2.10 p.m. on a sunny winter's day to fly east out toward the Bahamas and then north and west, completing a triangle flightpath that would bring them back to the Florida coast. In the course of the flight they would practise bombing over a small rocky cay.

Soon after they headed out to sea, the weather deteriorated and at 3.40 p.m. a flight instructor landing at Fort Lauderdale overheard Taylor talking to his most experienced student. The gist of this conversation was that both men thought they had made a wrong turn and Taylor, familiar with the Florida Keys near Miami, believed they were here and not over the very similar-looking and (to him) unfamiliar cays near the Bahamas. Taylor claimed his compass was not working. He was trying to persuade his team to fly north.

If Taylor was correct and they were over the Keys, this route would have brought them back to land. If, as seems virtually certain, he was wrong and they were over the Bahamas, this route would have been a big mistake. Flying north from the Bahamas would take the aircraft out over hundreds of miles of open Atlantic Ocean. At least twice afterwards, other listeners heard students suggesting to Taylor that they fly west, which would have brought them to the mainland, but he seemed convinced that he knew where the mission was, in which case a flight west from the Keys would be a tragic error.

Although attempts were made to establish direct contact, communications were poor that night and Taylor appeared unwilling to switch to an uncluttered emergency frequency because of his understandable fear that by so doing he might lose touch with his scattered and by now rather rattled young team of aircrew. They were his priority.

At 5.15 p.m. Taylor was heard to say that they were finally flying west, but when they failed to sight land (probably because they had flown so far out to sea they were now at least ninety minutes east of shore) he changed his mind again. At 6.04 p.m. he reported flying east. This confusion may well have caused the disaster that was looming.

The planes, of course, were rapidly running out of fuel and the sea had become choppy. It was also growing dark. Taylor was heard to order all craft to close up in tight formation and 'ditch' together as soon as the first one ran almost dry on fuel. After 7.04 p.m. nothing more was heard from them and no sign of any of the aircraft was ever found. One investigator added sardonically that they had vanished 'as completely as if they had flown to Mars' – ill-chosen words that were to be picked up by many in future.

Although nobody knew the exact position of Flight 19, several planes were sent to search the darkened seas for wreckage or survivors, even though it was known that an Avenger could not stay afloat for more than seconds in the weather that now pre-

vailed. Tragically, one of these rescue aircraft completely disappeared en route to a rendezvous point. It had no time to send a distress signal but a passing ship observed a huge explosion in mid-air and wreckage falling into the ocean. That rescue plane, a Martin Mariner, was notoriously rumoured to be susceptible to fuel leaks that could be ignited by the slightest spark. Their pilots named them 'flying gas tanks'.

Naturally, the total disappearance of all these aircraft and men within such a short time and in such a restricted area led to intense speculation. Certain comments by Taylor (e.g. that he did not know where he was) could easily be misinterpreted. Much later, it was alleged that words had been spoken in the (unrecorded) conversations between Flight 19 and Fort Lauderdale that included references to the sea looking 'strange' and a warning, 'Don't come after me! They look like...' (words trailing off). But no official source has ever verified the hearing of such transmissions and these words are not in the records of the accident enquiry.

That enquiry blamed Taylor's confusion over his position as the unfortunate cause of a genuine accident. Relatives disputed the finding, but it was upheld by a naval board. A legal battle ensued and in October 1947 this caused the US Navy to change its verdict to 'cause unknown'.

Although many see little reason to suppose the events to be mysterious, others insist that some weird force was responsible for the tragedy. Indeed, in 1977, Steven Spielberg's movie *Close Encounters of the Third Kind* actually had the planes found intact and working in the Mexican desert, the crews later being brought back to Earth as part of an exchange deal between a landed UFO and the US government's investigation team! On a more superficial level, a 1993 British TV advertisement for sugar-free drinks offered a different explanation, claiming that steam from exploding spy submarines caused similar planes to go off-course, with their crews ending up in a bar (doubtless consuming sugar-free drinks). In any event, the legend of Flight 19 lives on.

In 1991 it was thought that Flight 19 had at last been found. Five Avengers were traced on the seabed east of Fort Lauderdale and one even bore the same squad number as was carried by a plane from the fatal mission. But when the wreckage was surveyed, it turned out that these were earlier aircraft that had been junked into the ocean. Flight 19 is still missing.

1946 9 JULY

GHOST ROCKETS

Between May and September 1946, more than 1000 reports were made throughout Sweden, Norway and Finland of 'rockets' streaking across the sky, both at night and in daytime. Some were reputed to have crashed into lakes. The evidence warranted a major investigation.

The most immediate fear was that these could be experiments by Soviet scientists using 'V' bomb technology captured from the Germans at the end of the war. The Germans had launched devastating long-range missile attacks on London in this way and were believed to be only a year from developing inter-continental bombs that could have struck New York. The notion that the USSR had access to technology thought to have been destroyed as the Allies closed in on the Nazis was taken seriously. Not only did the Scandinavians probe the matter, but US and British enquiries were made as well. Some of the reports are still top-secret, but the theory of Soviet involvement was swiftly rejected.

On 9 July a photograph was taken of one of the pear-shaped 'ghost rockets' but it was interpreted, as were many other sightings, as a brilliant meteor. The wave of fast-moving lights is still unexplained.

1947

THE ARRIVAL OF THE FLYING SAUCERS

Hot on the heels of the mysterious ghost rockets, a new phenomenon was set to hit the world with a vengeance – flying saucers.

As with many aspects of the supernatural, this one can clearly be traced to a foregoing period (indeed the airships, phantom aircraft and ghost rockets may all be manifestations of the same phenomenon earlier in the century). But it was in June 1947 that it first received a name.

Once named, any mystery takes on a life of its own and starts to snowball. People have a hook to which they attach their own sightings and thus report them more freely than before. The media pay attention and collect data, because it sells. All of this generates more publicity and more reports and the mystery soon becomes a dynamic, unstoppable process.

Such mysteries are often fairly short-lived, running out of steam after a few months. The fact that the flying saucer mystery has survived for fifty years in such an extraordinarily resilient manner testifies to its unique features.

Between May and August 1947 the far-western states of America were hit by a wave of sightings of night lights and silver blobs in the daytime. The one that attracted most attention came from Kenneth Arnold on 24 June 1947 when flying over the Cascade Mountains in Washington State. He saw a group of objects skimming the clouds. They looked like crescent-shaped planes with swept-back wings, and he assumed they were secret aircraft built by the USA.

After mentioning this fairly low-key sighting to friends at a stop-over point on his route, he was greeted at his destination in Oregon by several reporters. A combination of factors, including a quiet news day, plus

Early reports of UFOs emphasized their saucer shape, and this is how they appeared in many subsequent photographs.

some of the sightings were described. In fact, they came in a wide variety of shapes and sizes, yet the concept of the classic disc- or saucer-shaped craft clearly stuck firm in the popular imagination and has never altered. That it was stimulated by a tabloid newspaper mistake is perhaps an ultimate irony, as the tabloids were to become absolutely essential in keeping the mystery alive during the decades to come.

Regardless of the faulty perception of what 'flying saucers' looked like, countless seemingly reliable reports flooded in, often from pilots and military personnel. They were sufficient for the army and air-force to take no risks and to mount an immediate joint enquiry into what it called 'Flying Discs'. The term UFO (Unidentified Flying Object) was also a military invention during the early 1950s by the successor to this initial study project.

Because the US government knew that it was not responsible for the discs or saucers, and with the previous year's events in Scandinavia (still largely secret) uppermost in mind, the programme to investigate the mystery was treated as a security priority on the assumption that these objects might be piloted by Soviet crews. If the USSR were capable of overflying the continental USA in such highly advanced craft, this would be a very serious matter for the White House. As such, the enforced cover-up was a perfectly responsible measure at that time.

Sadly, when enquiries rapidly ruled out the Soviets of all consideration, the practice of confiding the problem to military teams was too well established to be altered, as was the determination to keep all conclusions secret. Between 1948 and 1969 three major military investigations (Sign, Grudge and Blue Book) collated over 15,000 reports and it was not until 1976 that the Freedom of Information Act made much of this accessible. Some remains secret today. By the time it was possible to see what had been going on, the prejudices and attitudes about UFOs were too well engrained.

immediate coverage now provided by newspapers, radio and television, guaranteed that the story took off. Arnold, in fact, had never mentioned that the objects were saucer-shaped. He described their motion through the air as like a 'saucer skipping across water' (or as one might bounce a flattened stone across a lake or river). Whether misunderstood or appropriated, the term 'flying saucer' was invented by the press. This was the much-needed boost. Everyone in the USA immediately started to look for these things.

The problem was that most people, quite understandably, assumed that the objects looked like saucers; and that is exactly how

Most of the sightings of UFOs can be otherwise explained but a few still defy rational interpretation.

Although the USSR was rejected as the source of UFO flights, some other origin had to be found. Military people were trained to think that these lights were flying craft (as they appeared to be) and from some unknown intelligence (which seemed logical). This fostered the idea, briefly but never too seriously toyed with by US authorities, that the pilots came from another planet alerted by Earth's explosion of atomic weapons in 1945.

The image of an 'extraterrestrial hypothesis' (or ETH, as it is known) was seized upon by a former military man, Major Donald Keyhoe. He may well have possessed some inside knowledge that the US government itself considered this option. He published the evidence and stimulated belief in a cover-up of that official conviction, initially in a widely read magazine article (*True*, January 1950) and then, a few months later, in the first-ever book on UFOs.

There is little doubt that this linking of

the UFO mystery with the ETH was the single most important factor that has maintained its status. For throughout the 1950s mankind was striving to travel into space and during the 1960s and early 1970s this became a reality. Consequently, the continuous series of sightings in the world's skies came to be viewed as probable alien visits.

The US authorities, however, soon began to lose interest, realizing, as did other countries, that more than nine out of ten alleged UFO sightings were merely cases of mistaken perception of known phenomena such as aircraft and stars. The unexplained ones posed no threat, and probably never had done; but they had to be monitored just in case a potential enemy used the UFO sightings as a smokescreen to launch spy missions.

Yet although military circles acknowledged that these things must be flying craft from another intelligence, some very obvious clues were missed. These UFOs had not suddenly appeared in 1947. In fact, they had been observed as long as people had scanned the skies. The ancient Romans had reported them as 'fiery shields'. In medieval

times they had been 'dragons', and more recently they had been described as airships and ghost rockets. Their form had merely been altered by current awareness. And once they had been identified, incorrectly, as discs and saucers, many people saw them exactly as such. This indicated that their actual shape was much more vague and imprecise, and that their perceived form was moulded, as in previous incarnations, by popular beliefs and expectations.

It would be a long time before any of this was realized. Even today any opinion concerning UFOs that seems to contradict the extraterrestrial hypothesis is treated with suspicion and scepticism. Yet since 1980 there has been a groundswell of research tending to steer us away from acceptance of that simple, incredibly persuasive but incorrect explanation made in June 1947 toward a more realistic recognition that there is an interesting, if less exotic, phenomenon behind the UFOs.

ALIEN ENCOUNTERS

Wartime technology developed for military purposes was finally transformed for peaceful use. Prop-driven aircraft gave way to jet airliners and rocket ships were launched into Earth orbit. Communication around the planet was becoming almost instantaneous.

In the area of the supernatural, the demand for speed and immediacy of intelligence altered our perception of what was taking place. UFOs fitted neatly into the technological niche that obsessed the age—space travel—and received prominent exposure in the media.

People became aware of the importance of understanding phenomena such as extra-sensory perception and dreams. And the earliest experiments under hypnosis were conducted to unravel past lives.

1950  1959

1950

YOU CANNOT BE SIRIUS

Two highly respected French anthropologists, Marcel Griaule and Germaine Dieterlen, reported on the nineteen years they had spent living with the Dogon – a tribe of two million people in French Sudan, later Mali, West Africa. They had built up so much trust that the elders of these people had revealed to them many secret tribal rituals. The scientists obtained hard evidence that such belief systems dated back up to 10,000 years.

Most remarkable of these traditions was that the Dogon possessed extraordinary and advanced knowledge of astronomy. They knew, for example, that Saturn had rings, that Jupiter had four large moons, that the Milky Way was a spiral galaxy and that the Earth rotated on its axis. Since most of this knowledge had been revealed by science only in recent times, it could not have been handed down in stories through the millennia, as the Dogon alleged.

Yet there was an amazing explanation as to how this did indeed happen. The tribal elders said that their knowledge had been given to them by amphibious creatures from a planet in the Sirius star system who had landed in the nearby desert and lived with the Dogon during prehistoric times.

The Dogon offered precise descriptions of these Nommos (who bear a surprising resemblance to the merfolk of Earth mythology) and of the 'ark' (spacecraft) which landed and then semi-submerged in water to provide its inhabitants with a retreat each evening after spending the day on land.

Even more remarkable are the accounts that the Nommo gave the Dogon of the Sirius star system itself. This is the brightest star in the sky and one of the closest to Earth, just 8.6 light years distant. Yet only in 1844 did astronomers recognize its eccentricities of orbit, speculating (and proving eighteen years later) that it was due to a tiny, unseen companion star (now called Sirius B), which orbits around Sirius A. The second star is only three times the size of Earth but is incredibly dense. Because of its smallness and the immense light output generated by Sirius A, the orbit of Sirius B was not measured until some six years before Griaule and Dieterlen reached the Dogon encampment. And it was not until 1970 – twenty years after the Dogon revelations – that Sirius B was first photographed.

Sceptics, of course, disputing the idea that aliens from Sirius could have given the Dogon any of this knowledge, suggested that they obtained the information from visiting twentieth-century missionaries. This has been effectively refuted, however, by Robert Temple, who has made a detailed study of the legends and found too much in-depth, if circumstantial, evidence to make that tenable. In any case, Griaule and Dieterlen point out that they would surely have known of other such visits before them. The Dogon elders would need to have fabricated the legends and, moreover, the artefacts associated with their cosmology, dated by the anthropologists as several hundred years old, would also have had to be faked.

One such artefact, indeed, shows a map of the orbit of Sirius B around Sirius A which is unusually eccentric, and unlikely to have been produced simply by guesswork. It is, in fact, scientifically correct. The anthropologists dated this object as sixteenth-century – when not even the most advanced astronomers in Europe could have predicted such a pattern.

The truth about the aliens from Sirius may only ever be established if a third, much brighter, companion star is found in orbit. The Dogons claim that the Nommo arrived from a planet circling here. However, while the existence of Sirius C has been speculated, no such star has yet been discovered.

1950 II MAY

FIRST PHOTOGRAPH OF A UFO

The first well-attested photograph of a UFO was taken by Mr and Mrs Paul Trent, a farming couple from McMinnville, Oregon, USA. The object, disc-like with a flattened base, flew over their land at some distance, and they took two black and white shots of it before it disappeared. They made no subsequent attempt to make money from their evidence.

When the US government funded a study into UFOs carried out by scientists at the University of Colorado between 1967 and 1969, this was one of the few photographic cases that the sceptical team failed to identify. Indeed, the report (arguing that UFOs do not exist) concluded in this instance that this was one of the very few examples where all the evidence 'appear(s) to be consistent with the assertion that an extraordinary flying object, silvery, metallic, disc-shaped, tens of metres in diameter, and evidently artificial, flew within sight of two witnesses'.

More sophisticated methods, using computer enhancement developed by NASA's deep space programme, have since exposed many cases that look to be genuine, but are hoaxes. The McMinnville photographs passed these tests as well and are widely considered to be among the most persuasive pieces of evidence ever obtained that some UFOs are actual constructed objects of unknown origin.

There are, of course, many who dispute this, claiming the pictures are fabricated, and citing the shadows on the eaves of the outbuilding as being inconsistent with the time of day when the Trents claim they took these shots. That opinion, however, is firmly in the minority.

1950 SUMMER

MIRACLE PHOTOGRAPH

During the 1950-3 war in Korea, an aircraft flying on a routine mission over a mountain range took this photograph of an area of snow-covered rock. Many believe it to be the image of Christ giving blessing to the fight against Communism.

This pattern is known to science as a simulacrum. It is thought to be an accident of light and shade enhanced by the acknowledged desire of the human brain to perceive order in what is merely a random set of information.

1951

THE YETI

All over the world there are legends about creatures midway in appearance between human beings and apes. They are entirely covered in hair, of about the same size as humans, or slightly larger, walking on two legs and displaying a rudimentary level of intelligence. They also give out a horrible smell!

The legends associated with these creatures are so consistent that most who have studied the data feel certain that they are a genuine hidden species. Native Americans, who have reported the beast for centuries, particularly in mountainous woods in the north-west of the country, refer to it as Sasquatch, or more affectionately as 'Bigfoot', in reference to the huge footprints it leaves behind.

In the Russian mountains the animal is called the Alma and in Australia the Aborigines have long been familiar with the Yowie. Interestingly, the fur of the creature

Tracks of the Yeti, discovered at 4900 m (16,000 ft) near Bumthang Gompa, Nepal.

69

Above: Edmund Hillary and Sherpa Tensing on Everest.
Opposite: the Abominable Snowman in fiction.

seems to differ locally in colour just as the pigmentation of a human skin or animal coat varies according to environment or as natural camouflage. Thus the Alma has a light brown or orange coloration, matching the surrounding terrain, whereas the Sasquatch is said to be a darker brown.

Undoubtedly the best-known, however, and the first to be studied in detail, is the Yeti – the local name for the white- or grey-furred humanoid that has been reliably attested in the Himalayan mountains for centuries. Yeh-teh means 'rock thing'.

During the 1950s these peaks were the focus of great attention during the race to conquer Mount Everest. Members of several expeditions spent months in the snow-covered ranges and had various encounters with the strange creature. They described it first as the 'Abominable Snowman', but it was eventually realized that this stemmed from a mishearing of a phrase used by the Tibetans that actually translated as 'manlike creature that is not a man'.

It was members of the famous Eric Shipton expedition to the area in 1951 who first secured truly impressive evidence that there might be a genuine unidentified crea-ture up there. A single, but very intriguing, photograph was taken on the glacier at Menlung, of a footprint – three-toed, bigger than a large man's boot and resembling no known animal.

Since then there have been many sightings and photographs of tracks but little other hard evidence. The few Yeti scalps and hairs that have supposedly been recovered usually turn out to be from more mundane animals.

Sightings of the creature itself certainly exist. Sherpa Tensing, later to share the first successful ascent of Everest with Edmund Hillary, claimed to have seen one playing in the snow near a monastery in 1949.

In 1970 noted mountaineer Don Whillans, near Annapurna, heard a strange noise and next night, after finding tracks, watched a distant humanoid creature through binoculars for twenty minutes.

Other British mountaineers, including the late Pete Boardman (with whom I went to school and so can attest to his integrity),

have had very narrow escapes. He and Joe Tasker heard a large creature crashing about through their camp at 17,000 feet up Changabang in 1977. In the morning they found chocolate bars had been removed from their scattered belongings.

In July 1986, famous climber Reinhold Messner had a close-up sighting of one such creature when it emerged from behind a tree. Indeed, the celebrated English actor and climber Brian Blessed told me he was most impressed by Messner's story when we met early in 1993 as he was making final preparations for his attempt to become the oldest man to climb Everest. At the same time he hoped to start work filming a major round-the-world series compiling evidence for the reality of the 'man beast' in many different countries.

Meanwhile another fascinating case came to light. Julian Freeman-Attwood, leading a three-man expedition over a remote glacier in Mongolia, camped in a totally isolated spot at 4 a.m. on 12 June 1992. Only a couple of hours later the team emerged from their tent to find the virgin snow disturbed by a trail of heavy footprints leading past them and up into the desolation ahead. They were remarkably similar in appearance to those filmed by Shipton in 1951 and from the depth of impression suggested a creature larger and heavier than a human being.

Sceptics admit that such footprints look imposing but provide no real evidence of an unknown creature, being made by some normal species, such as a bear. Because they lie undisturbed for days or weeks, they are subject to considerable interference from the Sun, which can melt and enlarge prints to create an odd result, quite unlike the tracks originally laid down. Yet the footprints filmed by Freeman-Attwood were undoubtedly those of a huge unknown animal.

Traces of a Yeti were claimed to have been discovered in the Andes in 1956.

SPONTANEOUS HUMAN COMBUSTION

The idea of a human being turned into a heap of ash with horrific rapidity by some unknown fire source is a terrifying image. It has been given very little attention through the ages, probably as a result of fear.

Yet cases have been known for several centuries. In Victorian times, the noted story-teller Charles Dickens attended inquests and garnered evidence from several reputed instances. In those days the occurrence was often cited by fervent anti-drink campaigners and militant Church authorities as the result of divine retribution. It provided a wonderful scare tactic aimed at the ungodly, even though there never was any evidence that excess alcohol in the body was likely to make one susceptible to spontaneous combustion. Dickens, ever the topical popular author, wrote off one of his villains (the obnoxious Krook) in this decidedly unusual way in the course of his later novel *Bleak House*.

While isolated cases were reported afterwards, the subject first attracted serious attention in July 1951 with the baffling death of 67-year-old old Mary Reeser at St Petersburg, Florida, USA. The 'cinder woman', as she became known, literally turned from a healthy human being, when last seen late on the evening of 1 July, to nothing but a charred foot amidst a heap of ash before 7 a.m. the next morning.

The remarkable thing about Mrs Reeser's death, as is typical of other cases of spontaneous human combustion (SHC), is that the surroundings in her apartment were little damaged by flames. Fire and forensic experts who visit such sites are baffled by the fact that plastic tiles beneath the body do not even melt, that combustible materials in the room remain unsinged and that

ALIEN ENCOUNTERS

The calcified remains of Mary Reeser, the mysterious case of SHC discovered in 1951.

there is no evident localization of the incredible temperatures needed to turn human bone into powder.

The FBI were involved in Mary Reeser's case because of the possibility that she might have been killed and the body burnt deliberately to mask evidence of a crime. But this remains pure theory.

The sceptics' view is that SHC victims burn slowly over the course of many hours – with the bones acting as the wick and the human fat wrapped around them functioning in the same way as candle wax. Some spark sets it off (Mrs Reeser was last seen smoking after taking sedatives) and the heat is focused inward by this candle mech-anism. Unfortunately, despite several attempts by the doubters, no evidence has been gathered to support the claim that such a process can occur in human bodies.

Most significantly, crematorium special-ists are professionally shocked by pho-tographs taken of SHC victims. They say that they cannot achieve such comprehen-sive destruction of human bones and a body (being, in fact, two-thirds water) even in the ideal conditions at their disposal. For this to occur in a few hours inside an ordi-nary living room, they find hard to believe.

In Mary Reeser's case, having had access to detailed investigation reports carried out at the time, Peter Hough and I ascertained that there is considerable reason to suspect that the fatal fire occurred at around 4.20 a.m. and not many hours earlier as alleged

by the sceptics. Two hours is simply not long enough for the wick effect utterly to consume a human body, and this deduction, if correct, merely enhances the strange nature of this case.

An unexplained example of spontaneous human combustion in London, 1964.

In Britain alone, about one hundred unexplained fire deaths occur every year. According to forensic and fire brigade sources, while no cases are ever diagnosed as being due to SHC, that possibility is suggested in perhaps ten instances. If true, it may mean that a hundred or more people die this way throughout the world each year. Officially, however, SHC does not exist and practically no research is being conducted into its potential causes.

Theories as to what may lie behind the phenomenon, assuming it to be real, include the notions that electrical fields inside the human body can short circuit, that atomic chain reactions can generate phenomenal internal heat and that a deadly cocktail of chemicals can form in the gut as a result of Western society's poor dietary habits. The last might explain why SHC seems almost non-existent in animals and why there are few, if any, cases recorded outside the more developed nations, e.g. in African tribal cultures.

Either way, reports of SHC seem to be on the increase. In a data base that Hough and I compiled in 1990 there were eleven candidate cases globally in the 1950s, seven during the 1960s, thirteen from the 1970s and twenty-two in the 1980s.

1952

THE BERMUDA TRIANGLE: MYTH OR MYSTERY?

The Bermuda Triangle is the perfect example of what sceptics Larry Kusche and Paul Begg have called a 'manufactured mystery'. They believe it to be pure invention: a myth created in the late twentieth century. Both have devoted a great deal of serious effort to proving their case.

The concept first appeared in an article for *Fate* magazine in October 1952 when George Sand spoke of how a 'watery triangle bounded roughly by Florida, Bermuda and Puerto Rico' had apparently generated the inexplicable disappearances of countless ships and aircraft.

The 1945 events involving Flight 19 off the Florida coast was a major case in point, so widely misunderstood as to attain baffling proportions. It had led researchers to sift archives and newspaper files to find a deeper pattern. Once established, the notion of the existence of a catastrophe-laden triangle was difficult to dispel.

Sand did not popularize the mystery to any great extent, but the triangle was occasionally mentioned in the ensuing years, its shape and size always varying. Some authorities saw it as covering half of the Atlantic Ocean, as far northward and eastward as the coast of Ireland, making calculations meaningless.

It was the writer Vincent Gaddis who invented the phrase 'deadly Bermuda triangle' in a 1964 magazine article. Yet even he failed to capitalize on its full commercial potential. That was left to Charles Berlitz who, in *The Bermuda Triangle* (1974), summarized the data accrued until then. The book sold over five million copies around the world. More books, television documentaries and movies followed. Then the sceptics marched in and did a thoroughly effective job. They soon made it clear that the biggest mystery was why anybody thought there was a mystery in the first place.

It has now been well established that many of the supposedly inexplicable disappearances were no such thing. Once the records were checked, accident enquiries studied and weather data analysed, such incidents proved anything but baffling. This part of the ocean is one of the most heavily shipped areas in the world and hundreds of aircraft overfly it daily. The weather can suddenly whip up a storm and any debris from a capsized ship or crashed plane sinks rapidly into the inaccessible depths. By simple statistics, it is obvious there will be more disappearances here than in most other comparable expanses of ocean. Yet that alone proves nothing of real significance.

One of the most frequently cited cases, the disappearance of the Japanese freighter *Raifuku Maru* in 1925, is typical. Popular triangle legend has it that the last received message from the ship was 'danger like dagger – come quick!' This caused all manner of speculation as to what force resembling a dagger might have provoked her total disappearance, as happened immediately after the signal. But the enquiry at the time had revealed that the final message, severely distorted, possibly by an electrical storm, was actually 'Now very danger – come quick!' Poignant and tragic, but hardly mysterious.

In other instances there were widely reported storms, cargoes that were volatile or highly explosive, or other valid reasons why an accident might easily have occurred.

There have also been attempts to bring the triangle into the modern era, with suggestions that NASA has had trouble with telecommunications during shuttle flights when passing over the area. One satellite

The Bermuda Triangle prefigured twenty years earlier in Hyatt Verrill's The Non-gravitational Vortex.

JUNE

25 CENTS
IN CANADA 30 CENTS

AMAZING STORIES

Scientifiction
Stories by

A. Hyatt Verrill
John W. Campbell, Jr.
Edmond Hamilton

was alleged to have been affected by a mystery blackout whenever it overflew the triangle. The silence was found simply to be due to the fact that a recording tape was automatically rewound at this same point in every orbit!

The genuine puzzles that do exist appear to be associated with reported instances of electrical and magnetic inteference experienced by aircraft flying in this area. Some scientists think that an unusual natural electromagnetic vortex may occasionally manifest in certain places, and that this could be one of the most powerful.

Noted aviator Martin Caidan has reported that on one occasion, near Bermuda, as he flew into a cheesecake sky where sea and cloud blended into one, all his instrumentation failed. Fortunately he emerged from it before he became completely lost. His account is strikingly similar to the incident in 1928 of the sailor on the British oil tanker who entered a strange reality for some minutes as the vessel passed through the same area, although this occurred years before the triangle legend was born.

There is also a claim, though the story lacks verification, that a civilian aircraft landing at Miami disappeared from radar screens for ten minutes, and that when it touched down all clocks and watches on board the place were exactly ten minutes slow.

The Bermuda Triangle thus has a curious double life. Many people unfamiliar with the supernatural accept it as a genuine, well-established phenomenon. It still features in potboiler books, silly science fiction films and general media stories. Yet the majority of serious researchers into paranormal phenomena and, of course, the sceptical scientists who dismiss all supernatural tales, are for once both in agreement that, despite the occasional interesting event in the area, in truth there is in all probability no such thing as a deadly Bermuda Triangle.

1952 20 NOVEMBER

THE CREATURE FROM VENUS

George Adamski, who ran a food and drink stand on the slopes of Mount Palomar observatory in the USA, and had for some time written speculative fiction about life on other worlds, claimed to have established contact with a Venusian in the Californian desert. It resembled a human with long blond hair and used sign language and sketches made in the sand to explain its origin.

This was the first of a series of alien contacts and visits to planets in our solar system made by Adamski, all of which featured in several books over the next five years. He claimed to have seen trees and rivers on the Moon, a possibility not refuted until after his death. Adamski also bolstered his case with a number of photographs, said to be of disc-like 'scout ships' and cigar-shaped 'mother ships'. The media loved him for this and he attracted a wide following. Even thirty years after his death, the 'contactee' movement, which he effectively founded, enjoys strong support, particularly on the American west coast.

Analysis and computer enhancement of the Adamski photographs failed to establish that they were of large, structured craft, even though a more interesting piece of cine film of a 'scout ship', taken later by one of Adamski's disciples, still has its adherents.

Many other contactees followed, at first only in the USA but later in Europe. Several spiritual foundations emerged, based on the teachings of the aliens via these contacts. The Aetherius Society, for example, which was founded by a London taxi driver, today has thousands of sincere members and intelligent proponents in the USA and worldwide. The society utilizes 'prayer batteries' to channel positive energy from alien 'masters', such as Lord Aetherius, in order to prevent wars.

The CIA, which convened secretly in 1952 to discuss UFOs, later commented favourably on how the overt stories of the contactees had helped them achieve a task they had long sought to do themselves – to defuse serious scientific interest in alien contact via UFO sightings.

The climax of the contactee movement came in the late 1950s. Indeed, one of their members stood against Nixon and Kennedy for US President (but withdrew on advice from his communicating alien friends). He did this, he claimed, to ensure that Kennedy won and staved off a nuclear holocaust threatened by the coming Cuban missile dispute with the USSR.

1953

MEMORIES OF PAST LIVES

Hypnosis has been known for thousands of years and used for two centuries, often for mere entertainment, after it was popularized by Franz Mesmer. Initially it was little more than a party trick and was rarely the

One of Adamski's photographs of a 'mother ship' with scout ships emerging from it.

source of serious experiment to unlock the subconscious mind.

There had been sporadic reports from 1906 onward of people in a trance who allegedly relived an existence previous to their birth. By the 1950s the work of psychologists such as Sigmund Freud (unravelling the hidden meaning of dreams) and the still active Carl Jung (who had proved that human beings shared a collective unconscious containing race memories and other common motifs) had begun to point the way toward possible new developments. The chance eventually fell to an amateur researcher in Colorado, Morey Bernstein.

Between late November 1952 and early 1953 (when her husband cut them short) Bernstein conducted a series of tests with a 29-year-old local socialite, Mrs Virginia Tighe. The staggering results became the subject of a best-selling book and popular movie entitled *The Search for Bridey Murphy*.

Under hypnosis, Mrs Tighe, who had no Irish descent, 'regressed' to a life as Bridget

(Bridey) Murphy, born in Cork in December 1798. She was able to provide an amazingly detailed account of her family, marriage, everyday features of her life, names of local streets and shops, and of her death after falling downstairs, having moved over 250 miles to Belfast. She could even dance Irish jigs, sing songs and use a few Irish words in their correct usage from 150 years beforehand, even though some had since altered in meaning.

Sceptics who set off to Ireland to disprove the claim as pure fantasy received a surprise. Although certain facts were wrong and some were uncheckable (records of births were not kept from that far back and thus no real Bridey Murphy could be proven to have lived), others, such as the names of shops and the coins then in use, were all correct.

Debate settled upon exactly what kind of data could be produced by hypnosis. It was dimly recognized already that it could release information and memories hidden from the brain. But equally it could stimulate fantasy and role play.

There was a clear choice about the Virginia Tighe/Bridey Murphy case. Either this life was a real memory seeping through, possibly getting contaminated to some extent along the way, or the woman was inventing the whole thing without realizing it, the few correct facts being incorporated from books she had read in the past. This Mrs Tighe vigorously denied.

Eventually, a rival Chicago newspaper reported that Mrs Tighe had lived as a small child close by an Irish family called Corkell, the mother bearing the maiden name of Bridie. Mrs Tighe said she had never known of this fact. Yet the possibility that this had been the source of the information used unconsciously by Mrs Tighe was too strong for most to resist, even though some parts of the exposé were never verified. It is worth mentioning, too, that Mrs Corkell's son was an editor with the newspaper chain carrying the story.

Psychologists later established that the brain retains memory of almost everything it experiences and that, whereas this is normally inaccessible to conscious recall, a process called cryptomnesia can sometimes loosen the ties and allow some of it to bubble to the surface. Hypnosis was found to enhance the probability of cryptomnesia.

Research into such matters continued, with further past life regression experiments grabbing the popular imagination. Sceptics strongly challenged the whole concept of hypnosis untapping the wonders of the human brain. They cited several examples of similar rich memories of past lives having without doubt stemmed from novels read long ago or from snatches of conversation from childhood, of which the hypnotized subject had no conscious recollection. The doubters claimed by implication that all past life memories could be reduced to a fantasy built from such earlier experiences if more research were possible.

Of course, there were many who aimed to disprove this and who set about conducting further investigation with new enthusiasm. Moreover, the fact that more than half the world's population outside the Christian religion maintained a strong belief in the reality of past life fuelled the desire to prove the sceptics wrong. The battle lines were quickly drawn.

1954 21 OCTOBER

UFO ENCOUNTERS IN EUROPE

The UFO mystery suddenly outgrew its American roots with a series of dramatic encounters during one ten-day spell. France was the focal point of the wave but cases were also generated in Britain, Spain and Italy.

The sightings were particularly interesting for providing the first reliable reports of alien entities being seen close to UFOs. They often resembled humans, tall and with blond hair, similar to those mentioned by the contactee movement. The difference was that there was no urge here to indulge in metaphysics or to found societies.

In one typical case, at Ranton, England on 21 October, Mrs Jessie Roestenberg and her two young children hid under a table in fear as the UFO hovered outside with two fair-haired beings gazing dispassionately down at them out of a large picture window. Many cases such as this occurred in isolation from one another during this dramatic burst of activity.

These reports helped to re-establish the credibility of UFOs and, in particular, of the idea of alien contact.

LIFE AFTER DEATH

Scottish medium Helen Duncan holds a particularly memorable place in the history of the paranormal for a number of reasons.

By 1956 she had had a controversial career spanning more than twenty-five years as a rare practitioner of the visible art of Spiritualism – being what is called a physical medium. She did much more than simply pass on messages received inside her

Medium Helen Duncan had many brushes with the law but was never proved guilty of fraud.

ALIEN ENCOUNTERS

mind from unseen spirits of the dead. Sticky white ectoplasm extruded from her body and allegedly formed into shapes of various dead relatives whom her clients were trying to contact. Their three-dimensional forms then briefly emerged from a cabinet, wandered into the dimly lit seance room, and departed again.

Countless people were convinced by all of this, later coming forward to attest to the authenticity of the apparitions they had seen and even touched. Some of the photographic evidence, however, looked less than persuasive. The materialized form of Mrs Duncan's 'child spirit guide', filmed at a seance in 1933, had the decided appearance of a blown-up doll with rather crudely painted facial features, wrapped in a white sheet. Be that as it might, such was the conclusion reached by the far from sceptical ghost hunter Harry Price.

Mrs Duncan had first been in trouble in 1933 when police infiltrated a seance in Edinburgh and she was charged with fraud. A policewoman grabbed at the ectoplasmic form and came away with a white vest! Witnesses to the seance signed a statement to this effect that was used in evidence at the trial. The medium was found guilty of deception and fined £10.

Later, during the war, when she began working in Portsmouth, England, the police mounted further raids. She was alleged to be a nuisance to the authorities because at one seance a sailor who had gone down with his ship came through and told of his recent death, but accused the Royal Navy of deliberately holding back public knowledge of the sinking. There was speculation that the medium had been given a hard time to prevent her accidentally discovering more war secrets!

When the police broke in on another seance in January 1944, their attempt to lay hold of ectoplasm and provide hard evidence for fraud failed. Even so, Mrs Duncan was arrested, held in jail and tried at the Old Bailey in a case that made national headlines. Although fraud and conspiracy to defraud were the main charges levelled against her, the 200-year-old Witchcraft Act was also cited (for the last time in British history). Despite testimony from supporters and an offer to give a demonstration in court, which the jury rejected, Helen Duncan was found guilty and sent to Holloway women's prison in London for nine months.

She emerged a broken woman, vowing in future to give up holding seances for money. But she was soon back in business. Meanwhile, popular outcry from the Spiritualist movement had caused the Witchcraft Act to be repealed. It was replaced by the Fraudulent Mediums Act.

In November 1956 Helen Duncan (now aged 58) held a seance in Nottingham that was staked out by police. Again they attempted to grab ectoplasm which they presumably expected to be some kind of normal material. To their astonishment, the medium collapsed.

Mrs Duncan was taken back to Scotland and entered hospital, seriously ill and reputedly bearing scorch marks on her stomach area, supposedly caused by the ectoplasm shooting back too fast into her body. Spiritualists had long claimed that shocking a medium out of a trance could be potentially fatal. Sadly, in this case, Helen Duncan may have proved them right. She never recovered and died suddenly five weeks later, officially from natural causes.

1957 16 OCTOBER

ALIEN BABIES

The world's first recorded (and consciously recollected) abduction by aliens allegedly occurred to 23-year-old farm worker Antonio Villas Boas near São Francisco de Sales, Brazil. He said that a strange object had descended out of the early morning skies and stopped his tractor engine dead.

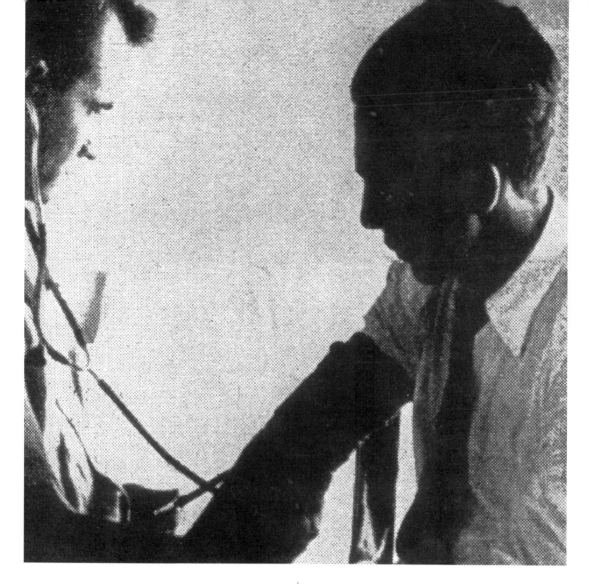

He was grabbed by several medium-sized men of human appearance wearing silvery suits and bundled into their domed landing craft. Inside he was rubbed down with a gel substance and tended by a strange female humanoid with red hair, who barked and yelped like an animal. The sexually aroused Villas Boas was then 'raped' by the woman who gestured to indicate that her purpose was to have his baby in outer space!

In January 1958, Dr Olavo Fontes conducted a full investigation and documented details. Villas Boas never made any money nor did he gain immediate publicity from the incident. Fontes decided to sit on the case, which was unprecedented, in the

Antonio Villas Boas undergoing medical tests following his alleged abduction by aliens.

hope that another like it might occur. Two similar incidents would then serve to confirm each other as proof of a real alien programme on Earth, presumably with the view of creating hybrid human/alien babies.

In 1961, details of the happening were submitted to the British UFO journal, *Flying Saucer Review,* but not published by the magazine for three years. Meantime the 'wild story' was vindicated by the events in New Hampshire (see 1961).

Less than five weeks after the Villas Boas encounter, however, a world away in the

83

English West Midlands, Cynthia Appleton, a young mother from Aston in Birmingham, had an equally dramatic encounter.

On 18 November 1957 the 27-year-old woman suddenly noticed that the sky had turned pink. Simultaneously, there was an electric flash in her living room (scorching the floor and a newspaper) and a tall, blond-haired figure materialized. He showed her a hologram (a concept not yet invented) and during the course of seven more visits up to early 1959 discussed science and philosophy with her.

In early June 1959 Cynthia gave birth to a fair-haired boy. Although it was apparently fathered by her husband (who never met the alien), Cynthia was convinced that the child's 'spiritual' pedigree was alien. She claimed that full details of the birth had been predicted during the final visit by the tall, blond stranger and that she had been told to name the baby Matthew.

When she first reported this story, the Villas Boas case had been recorded in Dr Fontes's surgery but had not been publicly revealed. In the month between the Brazilian adventure and Mrs Appleton's first alien contact, the Earth had entered the space age, with the Soviet launch of Sputnik 1. Moreover, an extraordinary sequence of events had occurred between 30 October and 7 November, when no fewer than thirty-three cases of car stoppages had been recorded, mostly in the western USA and nine of these within the Levelland, Texas, area on the night of 2/3 November alone. This amazing cluster of events within such a short time represented one-third of all such known cases during the decade up to 1957.

In such instances, a UFO, usually in the form of a glowing ball of energy, appears in front of a car and causes a complete loss of power, stopping its engine and extinguishing its headlights. A strong electrical field seems to be generated and various theories have attempted to identify this. Those who support the idea that UFOs are alien visitors claim it as a demonstration of superior

technology to show ways that these visitors could destroy our civilization.

It is certainly intriguing, even though most of the cases happened in isolation from one another and were free of any likely collusion, that this combination of strange events occurred at such an appropriate point in Earth history. The wave was sandwiched between two incidents that likewise involved powerful electrical fields – stalling the farmer's tractor and burning the mother's floor. Neither achieved publicity at the time yet both featured a new theme – of 'alien babies' – a trend that was to become dominant decades later.

1958 4 OCTOBER

THE REBORN TWINS

After five or six years of research into the possibility of reincarnation, arguments still raged as to the unsuitability of evidence procured under regression hypnosis. Then a case occurred which seemed to provide the perfect answer to the critics.

It did not come from a country such as India, where belief in past-life existence was commonplace. Nor was hypnosis involved in any way. The memory was completely conscious and, indeed, even displayed some associated physical evidence.

The events began tragically in England on 5 May 1957 when two sisters, aged 6 and 11, the only children of the Pollock family from Hexham, Northumberland, were killed along with a young male schoolfriend in a freak accident. A widow, who had taken an overdose of sleeping pills and was determined to end it all at the wheel of her new car, careered down the hill and struck the three children as they walked cheerfully along the pavement toward a church service. They were killed outright.

John Pollock, despite being a Catholic, had a strong and rather unusual belief in reincarnation, a doctrine not accepted by his faith. He had prayed repeatedly for this to be proven through him in some way. After the tragedy, and apparently without the agreement of his wife, Florence, he came to see this terrible event as punishment for his pleas to God; but he also felt sure that the matter was not at an end and that his prayers would be answered.

Some months later, Florence became pregnant. John announced that she would give birth to twins and that they would be the couple's dead daughters reincarnated. Florence, horrified by this notion, openly scoffed. Her doctor was adamant that as there was no history of twins in either family the chances were highly remote. The hospital gynaecologist added that only one foetus was detected in Mrs Pollock's womb. End of argument.

Yet Florence Pollock did after all give birth to twin girls on 4 October 1958 – just seventeen months after the tragic death of their sisters.

Immediately, it was noticed that one twin had a faint white mark on her forehead that matched a scar on the head of one the dead daughters after she had fallen from her bicycle as a toddler.

There was also a birthmark on the hip of that same newborn daughter, exactly where it had been on her dead sister. Such birthmarks may pass from generation to generation, yet it was considered unusual that, despite the twins being formed from just one egg, which normally means they are identical and share all major physical characteristics, only one of them possessed that birthmark. The same, of course, had been true of the deceased (non-twin) sisters. Although the forehead scar faded after a few years, the birthmark remained.

Various incidents occurred to confirm John Pollock's opinion that his dead daughters had been reborn. The family moved from Hexham when the babies were only a few months old, but he brought them back for a single day (at the age of three) on advice from a reincarnation expert in the USA. Inevitably, motivation must to some extent have coloured the reported results. Nevertheless, John Pollock said that the girls unmistakably recognized things (e.g. the school attended by their dead sisters) that they certainly ought not to have known about.

When the girls were four, some dolls were left outside their room. These had belonged to their sisters and had been locked away for the past five years. Although the subject of reincarnation had never been mentioned in the twins' presence (at their mother's insistence), they might admittedly have overheard their parents discussing it. Either way, both girls reportedly recognized these dolls, gave them the correct names and identified which belonged to which sister from their supposedly previous existence.

More frightening still were the occasions when one sister was found cradling the other, talking about blood pouring from her mouth, just as it had after the terrible accident; or when both girls were found in the back garden clutching each other tightly, screaming out loud, after a car had started up and happened to be pointing toward them at the same angle as the car that had killed their sisters during their final, terrifying moments.

After the age of 5 years these incidents ceased. The twins did not learn of their supposed reincarnation until 1972 and both grew up with no way of knowing whether or not it was credible. They had no conscious memory connecting them with their long-dead sisters. As adults, one took an interest in the paranormal, the other preferred to avoid talking about the matter altogether.

Like the rest of us, the Pollock girls may never know whether their experience was a strange psychological mystery, somehow connected with their father's unusual beliefs, or whether they really were brought back from death to the family that they had lost, as amazing proof of eternal life.

THE SPACE RACE

During the 'Swinging Sixties' a continuous stream of new technology—for example, transistors that miniaturized electronics to startling effect—almost concealed the day-to-day improvements now taken for granted. The decade was significant, too, for its exploration on two fronts—what might be termed inner and outer space.

America's near-miraculous achievement of landing men on the Moon defied even the best scientific commentators of the day. As for inner space, this was the era when the limitations of our knowledge of the human psyche were first truly appreciated. Consequently, there was an explosion of interest in the workings of the mind, in altered states of consciousness, reaching out into other dimensions, and a reawakening of spiritual values.

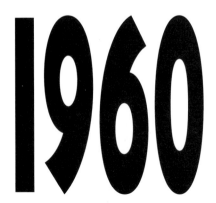 

1960

VOICES IN THE SKY

Ever since the discovery of radio waves, it had been speculated that if ESP was a similar form of energy, as was thought probable, then some kind of instrument might be devised that could tune into other dimensions. A prime candidate for this concept was the realm of life after death.

In the late summer of 1959, Friedrich Jurgenson, a Swedish film producer who specialized in nature recordings, was taping bird songs when on playback strange sounds intruded into his work. They seemed to be voices from thin air talking in snatches about the very subject he was recording.

Despite this odd coincidence, Jurgenson assumed that his microphone had picked up a stray radio transmission that chanced to be on that topic. Throughout 1960 he tried many more experiments and the voices kept appearing: always faint and speaking in short bursts at what seemed to be 'speeded up' rates. But often, once he had attuned to them, they were unmistakably human voices. Moreover, he sometimes recognized them as dead friends or relatives.

By the mid-Sixties, the progressive German government had funded parapsychological research at the University of Freiburg, under the directorship of Professor Hans Bender. He was one of the first to take an interest in Jurgenson's work, followed swiftly by Dr Konstantin Raudive, a psychologist exiled from the former Latvian republic before its annexation by the USSR. Raudive taped hundreds of voices in ten years of experiments that culminated in his 1971 book *Breakthrough*, which first introduced the mystery to the English-speaking world.

Research into what came to be called EVP (electronic voice phenomenon) now began in earnest, with new methods being sought to improve the quality of communication. Although many workers felt certain that this was technological proof of life after death, Bender himself inclined to the theory that the mind of the experimenter was somehow altering the magnetic fields imprinted on to the audio tape and creating the voice patterns by using so-called PK (psychokinesis) – the same force believed to trigger poltergeist activity. Certainly the voices were 'real'. Tests with carefully screened equipment in sealed rooms proved positive, and they yielded voice print readings on an oscilloscope, in the same manner as any speech pattern.

When Raudive died in 1974, his 'voice' was recorded a few days later. He seemed to be pleading that work should continue and 'other techniques' be explored. Even better results were subsequently claimed by using special circuitry or by recording on to demagnetized tape from 'white noise' static off the radio band when carefully tuned away from any transmitting stations.

It was this final step that was eventually to provide the most amazing of all alleged communications. But that was not until 1977.

1961

THE LIFE FORCE

Dr Semyon Kirlian was an electrical engineer in the USSR. In 1939 he discovered by accident an effect not understood for several more years.

Kirlian was using a high-voltage system to generate low current in his laboratory, investigating the possible effects of energy fields on the health and wellbeing of animals. As his hands moved alongside the electrode, a flash of light lit the room. He was briefly struck by a blast of energy; but the current, unlike that given out during a thunderstorm, was not strong enough to be dangerous. Kirlian wondered, nevertheless,

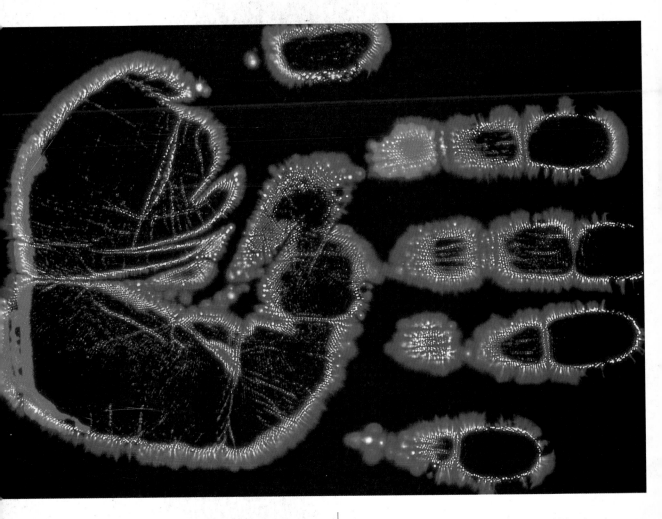

what might have happened had that instantaneous flash been frozen on to film. So he tried to duplicate the process by using light-sensitive paper. The result was a weird picture of his fingertips with brightly coloured streaks of energy pouring from them. It rather resembled the photosphere of the Sun when filmed during an eclipse.

In 1961 this work was imported to the West in the wake of new knowledge about biological energy fields found to be surrounding living creatures. Weak electrical and magnetic fields were known to be generated. It emerged that some animals, notably birds, used them to navigate by inter-reacting with the much stronger electro-magnetic fields of the Earth itself. This

Kirlian photographs of the palm of a human hand (above) and of the fingers of a healer (opposite). The technique has aroused keen interest and controversy.

gave a new incentive to so-called Kirlian photography.

At first it was assumed, particularly in Spiritualist circles, that these pictures had captured the 'aura' generated by the spirit body of a living creature. Unfortunately, it proved to be no such thing. Kirlian images can be taken of inanimate objects, and the bright colours that characterize the photographs of hands and leaves (readily adaptable Kirlian subjects) are a controllable product of the photographic technique and not of the object being filmed.

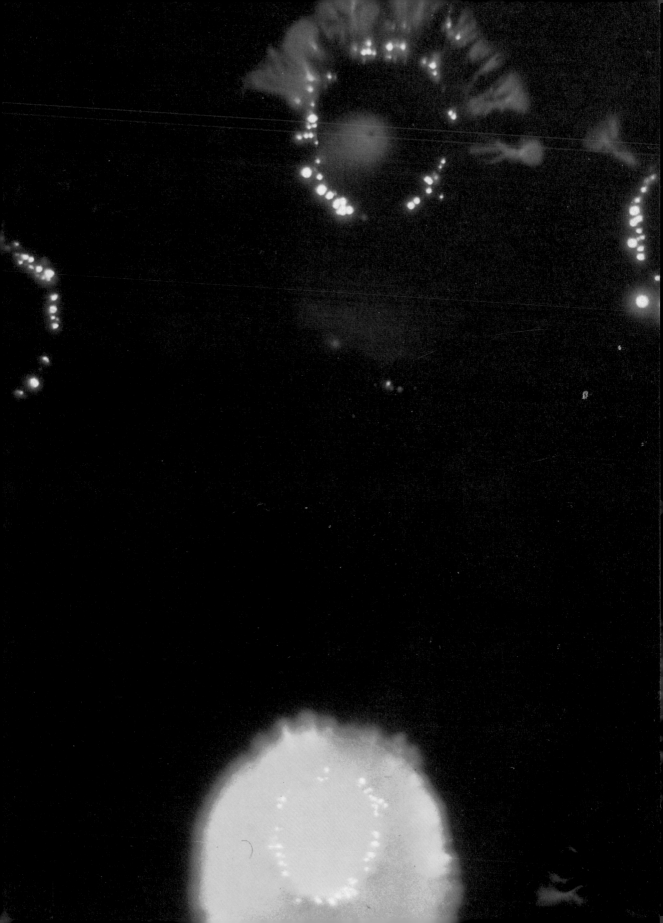

Some evidence was accumulated that the Kirlian 'aura' altered according to the state of health of the subject involved. Dr Thelma Moss, at the University of Rochester, New York, established marked differences, for example, between Kirlian photography of rats with cancer and rats without the disease. But some of this was eventually shown to be a result of chemical body changes which produce a different electrical reaction, making the photography a useful diagnostic tool but not a supernatural one.

However, there are some stranger claimed results. In experiments with leaves, a few photographs have revealed what appears to be the whole leaf even after part of it has been torn away – as if an after-image of the aura remains. Those who support the view that the Kirlian photographs depict some kind of life field surrounding all objects (inanimate objects allegedly picking these up by contact with living things) maintain that this field does not disperse when the physical body dies, thus offering some evidence for survival of death. They cite, as possible further evidence of this invisible energy field, cases in which amputees lose limbs but can 'feel' their presence long after the surgery is concluded.

Biologist Dr Rupert Sheldrake extended the concept later still with his research into what he called the 'morphogenetic' (or M) field – essentially a structuring energy field that surrounds all genetic material. He felt that this serves as a blueprint to ensure that physical cells grow into the correct form rather than anything else. Although such life energy has many similarities with the Kirlian aura, Sheldrake did not develop his work from that premise, progressing to much more sophisticated concepts about how these M-fields adapt and change as time goes by. Thus he was actually defining a psychological, spiritual and psychic theory of evolution to parallel the purely physical process treated by Darwin. As

such, his book, *New Science of Life*, was hailed a candidate for burning by much of mainstream science and remains anathema to many of his colleagues, even though he has worked hard to devise experiments to prove or disprove his thesis.

Kirlian photography undoubtedly works through a perfectly understood natural physical process called the 'corona discharge', in which the air between the filmed object and photographic material breaks down and ionizes into its constituent parts through an electrical burst of energy. What is in doubt is whether the pictures that result are merely random effects of this mundane process or some aspects of a hidden energy field surrounding a human body. Is it illuminated into brief perspective just as a lightning flash can make the landscape visible for a fraction of a second?

1961 19 SEPTEMBER

THE WHITE MOUNTAINS ABDUCTION

The first major spacenapping (alien abduction) to achieve global attention occurred in the White Mountains of New Hampshire, USA, late this night.

Betty Hill, a social worker, and her husband, Barney, were driving home from a Canadian holiday when they observed a white light in the sky. A local air force base recorded an unidentified radar tracking at the same time. The couple watched through binoculars and then suffered a curious 'time loss', arriving home with no memory of part of their journey.

They reported the incident immediately, but were troubled by its missing aspects. Betty was dogged by strange dreams and eventually they both visited a doctor. After doing the rounds of the medical profession, they ended up at the Boston offices of psychiatrist Dr Benjamin Simon. Between

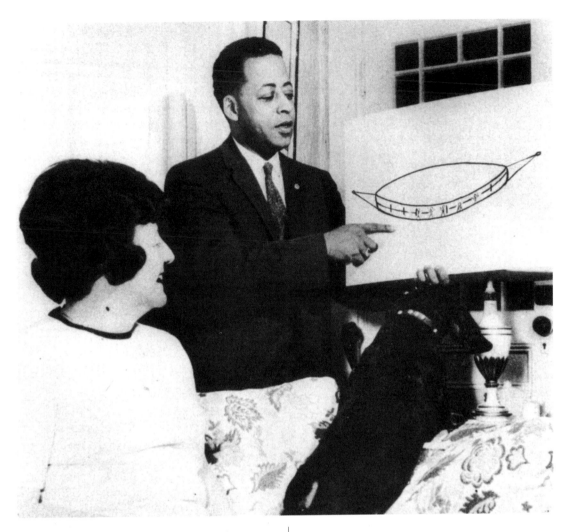

December 1963 and June 1964 he conducted numerous hypnotic regressions to relieve the anxiety of the couple. To his amazement, the treatment uncovered the memory of a supposed spacenapping.

In these sessions both the Hills described being taken aboard a landed object by small creatures with large eyes and pasty skins and given detailed medical examinations. Betty had a pregnancy test, with a long needle used to draw ova samples (a technique not then in use but later adopted in test-tube baby research). Barney had sperm samples sucked into a tube placed over his groin. The couple were also shown a complex 'star map' that located the alien world

Spacenapping victims Betty and Barney Hill with a sketch of the spacecraft they claim to have encountered.

as a planet around the star Zeta Reticulii (according to calculations by astronomy teacher Marjorie Fish, based on Betty Hill's hypnosis testimony). They tried to take a book as proof of the events but the aliens, apparently after some debate, decided not to allow this.

Dr Simon did not believe in the actual reality of these hypnosis memories. He accepted that the Hills believed them and that this was not a fraud, but considered it to be a delusion. The couple sought no publicity, were clearly perturbed and spent

THE SPACE RACE

Car travellers encountering UFOs have sometimes recollected abductions during hypnosis sessions.

a good deal of their own money on therapy in an attempt to overcome the trauma. Nevertheless, the story somehow leaked out in 1965 (though the Hills were apparently not responsible). In due course local journalist John Fuller persuaded them to let him tell their story in a classic book, *The Interrupted Journey,* which was serialized throughout the world and was later adapted as a faithful and sober TV movie *(The UFO Incident).*

Much of this material, of course, was already documented before 1964 when the Villas Boas case was published in England, even though that incident had been on record since 1958. The parallels, including entity descriptions, techniques used and interest in human reproduction, seem hard to dismiss.

1962 12 AUGUST

LAKE MONSTERS

The first serious rival to Nessie's supremacy was a major photograph of the monster said to live in Lake Manitoba in Canada. The very unusual shot was captured by two fishermen in a motorboat and it depicts a snakelike object almost on top of the water. The men estimated its size as about 10-12

feet and compared it to a gigantic eel, moving in typically sinuous fashion. They attempted to give pursuit but despite the speed of their vessel could not catch it before it sank from view.

Many of the Great Lakes on both sides of the US/Canadian border have traditions of monsters. Massive sturgeon up to 10 feet long have been reported and these fish, which can survive for up to fifty years, have sometimes been held responsible for such stories. Native Indian legends and sightings by trappers dating from long before Loch Ness was popularized describe these unknown serpent-shaped creatures with romantic names such as Ogopogo (in Lake Okanagan) and Champ (Lake Champlain).

1964 24 MAY

THE GHOST IN THE WHITE SUIT

Jim Templeton, a fire officer in the northern English city of Carlisle, went out with his family on a sunny spring day to a beauty spot on the nearby marshes of Solway Firth. At one point he took some colour photographs of his daughter Elizabeth holding a bunch of flowers. He could hardly have predicted the outcome when the film was processed. Jim was told that it was a pity his best shot had been spoiled by the man standing in the background. Yet no such man had been there.

Examination of the print shows something extraordinary. A semi-transparent figure can be seen standing behind Elizabeth's head. Yet it is set at a slanting angle, in such a way that it would be floating a few feet off the ground if viewed in full perspective.

However, this is unlike any normal phantom photograph. The 'ghost' appears to be wearing a space suit!

In fact, the white clothing and visor are more akin to a radiation protection suit or, appropriately, considering Mr Templeton's occupation at the time, a fireman's silver uniform for dealing with special hazards.

Aside from Mr Templeton, his wife and their other daughter, who were standing close by when the photograph was taken, were equally sure that nobody intruded into the shot. They did notice, however, that the air was 'charged' as if an electrical storm were brewing. Sheep and cows near by were behaving oddly as if in response to that.

The matter was reported to the police, who tried to suggest it was a streaker, but admitted the Templetons would have noticed someone running around the marshes without any clothing. They also considered a double exposure, with another of the Templeton negatives – perhaps of a colleague in a firesuit – accidentally stamped on top of this shot during laboratory processing. Kodak, however, examined the film and concluded otherwise, noting that there was no overlap of the figure in the girl's hair – where the double exposure would have continued if this was how the effect were produced. The image appeared to be of a semi-transparent but real person partially blocked out by the back of the girl's head.

Supernatural theories have included a Japanese researcher's idea of a holograph projected by chance through electrical fields, perhaps from the Chapel Cross nuclear power plant across the Solway Firth. If so, it must have been projected through time as well as space because the plant authorities stated they had no men working in protective suits on that day. Alternatively, a UFO expert suggested a partly formed alien entity emerging from an otherwise invisible craft.

The incident apparently aroused government interest, for a few days later two men in a dark car, showing identification, quizzed Jim Templeton at the site, asking peculiar questions about bird life. They became annoyed when he refused to accept that he had not filmed an ordinary man, and drove off leaving him to hike the five miles home! The Ministry of Defence denied any knowledge of this interview.

The only mundane options left were an unspecified 'freak picture', as the police eventually decided, or a combination of drying marks in the development that by chance resembled a figure, something Kodak thought very improbable. The company offered a reward of free film for life to any photographic expert who could solve the mystery. Thirty years later the reward is unclaimed.

1965

THE OUTER SPACE FRONTIER

Throughout the 1960s, both the USA and USSR launched dozens of manned flights into Earth orbit and then onward to the Moon. There were countless other remote probes to film the Moon, Mars and Venus.

The Moon's influence on zodiacal signs and human lives, as depicted in a 15th-century book on astronomy.

Inevitably, during some missions, strange things were seen. But were any of them truly unexplained?

In a detailed review of the evidence published in 1969, Dr Franklin Roach, an astrophysicist at the University of Colorado and a NASA consultant, picked out three experiences that had some curious features.

Two of these occurred during a Gemini 4 flight in June 1965 and involved astronaut James McDivitt. The most interesting was an object like a beer can with protruding antennae that he saw as the craft orbited over Hawaii on 4 June. He took film of this, but when NASA released what they assumed were his shots, he was convinced that the two white and rather fuzzy blobs were not what he had seen but were reflections of sunlight off bolts on the capsule's window. Despite an extensive search through the thousands of images that were taken on that mission, the actual pictures of the object were never traced. Although McDivitt does not think that sinister, assuming that his hasty photography of a briefly perceived object did not turn out as well as expected, he nevertheless believes that the unidentified object he saw was probably orbiting material and not an alien spaceship astride Gemini 4.

In December 1965, James Lovell and Frank Borman, two astronauts who participated in subsequent Moon missions, engaged in a recorded conversation with ground control, describing a 'bogey at 10 o'clock high'. This was confirmed not to be a booster rocket from their own launch (which tended to remain close to capsules and cause spurious sightings). They saw one large, unidentified light and many smaller particle lights near by.

In other flights, e.g. Gemini 12 on 12 November 1966, film was taken of strange objects in the form of large blobs. Although not definitely identified, sceptics think them unlikely to be mysterious. Indeed, some of them appear to be debris cast out into orbit from the tiny spacecraft – including bags of waste matter. These reflect the unfiltered sunlight so strongly that they can glow with great intensity.

The most persistent legends, however, have grown up around the Apollo flights to the Moon which followed these Gemini 'dry runs'. Several ham radio operators claim to have heard the 'real' broadcasts from Neil Armstrong and Buzz Aldrin while on the Moon's surface in July 1969, rather than those relayed by NASA after a slight delay to allow any security data to be 'blacked out' from transmission to the watching world.

According to these utterly unsupported allegations, the crew of Apollo 11 spoke of being met on the Moon, describing what they saw in terms such as, 'These babies are huge, sir... Oh God, you wouldn't believe it! I'm telling you there are other spacecraft out there ... lined up on the far side of the crater.'

I have myself heard these stories directly from alleged earwitnesses, but they have no hard evidence (e.g. tape recordings) to back them up. NASA, of course, denies any truth to them, adding that it relayed most of the Apollo 11 messages from the Moon in real time and would have been glad to tell the world had it found evidence of alien life.

Then in 1979 the former chief of NASA communications, Maurice Chatelain, published his extraordinary book, *Our Ancestors Came from Outer Space*. In the main this followed a trend after the rapid termination of the Moon landings in 1973, suggesting that their unexpected ending was not due to financial cutbacks (as the US government insisted) but to the alien presence they had discovered on the Moon's surface. He alleged that the gist of the Apollo 11 story was correct. There were indeed strange craft on the Moon; although Armstrong and Aldrin have never supported such allegations.

More stories of such a presence came from George Leonard, a researcher who scrutinized detailed photographs of the

lunar surface and claimed to be able to see machines carrying out mining operations, together with artificial structures. Few could find these things in his photographs, despite circles pointing out where to look, but he stressed that you needed to stare at the pictures to adapt your eyes and then the fine details emerged.

Not surprisingly, most scientists thought that eyestrain was a more likely explanation for this effect. They noted that the famous 'canals' observed on Mars a century ago eventually turned out to be mundane geological features too small to be seen even through the best Earth telescopes. Imagination 'joined the dots' to see evidence of structure and intelligence that was never really there. The same effect may well be at work with the orbital shots of Moon craters containing alien heavy plant machinery.

Even in the 1980s the claims of strange encounters during spaceflights persisted. A

An artificial structure supposedly found on close-up shots of the lunar surface. A sign of alien presence or a rock shadow?

shuttle flight in March 1989 was supposedly involved in a close encounter with an 'alien spacecraft' while on a military mission in Earth orbit. Those exact words actually appear on a tape of the ground-to-space communications that reached the tabloid press. At the same time it was alleged that a 'fire' had been reported on board the shuttle, but that 'fire' was actually a code word for alien contact!

Careful investigation by UFOlogists revealed that this story fell apart. The crew were very helpful and gave full and frank statements. The tape that circulated was reported to be a recording of a hoax message from an unknown source breaking into a relay frequency used by NASA.

If true, even the tricksters are becoming more sophisticated.

95

Sightings of wild cats, assumed to be long extinct in Britain, continue to be reported.

1966 14 AUGUST

MARAUDING FELINES

There are many claims that wild cats, akin to jungle pumas or panthers, are still at large in various parts of the world where they are supposedly extinct. Although reports from the USA or Australia, where similar animals were around until quite recently, may not be all that surprising, it is much more controversial in a country such as Britain, where it is thousands of years since any such animals roamed what was then a very different habitat.

Yet the sightings are extensive, with focal points of activity in south central Scotland, the Pennine Hills in northern England and, in particular, the moorland areas of Devon and Cornwall. Here unknown beasts have been blamed for killing sheep, but man-hunts have failed to ensnare them.

In the mid-1960s a wave of big cat sightings occurred in Surrey and a rare photograph was obtained by a police officer at Worplesdon near Guildford. The cat, said to resemble a puma, was only yards away.

Opinion is divided as to what these creatures are. Some believe they are merely large domestic cats gone feral (wild). On other occasions dogs are mistaken if the conditions are not ideal. There are also some recorded instances of big cats kept as pets escaping from their owners and roaming free. But if the sighting numbers are anything to go by, a whole colony of big cats must be at large; yet no carcasses or bones have been discovered.

1967

MYSTERY MUTILATIONS

On 15 September 1967, a three-year-old pony called Snippy was found dead in Alamosa County, Colorado. The loss of a pet was a family tragedy, but it was the manner of death that was to have major repercussions.

Snippy was found partly skinned, its throat cut with what appeared to be a surgical instrument. Body organs had been removed, as if during a skilled operation, and all the blood was drained. Yet no mess had been caused. There was not a drop of blood on the ground by the body.

The police investigation failed to come up with a solution, but there were those who noticed that it had occurred amid a major wave of UFO sightings worldwide. Indeed, during the last week in October, Britain had its biggest ever outbreak of sightings, leading to questions in Parliament and a government decision (still applicable) to retain all documentation in official channels.

Other mutilations followed, mostly involving cattle in Colorado, Wyoming, Texas and other mid-western states of the USA. Theories normally settled on a Satanic rites cult, but several major investigations failed to find any support for this. The most active mutilation centre outside of the USA was Puerto Rico, where voodoo was still practised by certain groups, so the idea was never totally rejected.

As time went by, and further cases emerged of surgically precise mutilation with bloodless wounds, it was suggested that laser beams might be instrumental; and researchers compiled evidence that strange, unmarked helicopters were frequently seen at sites near by. Were they carrying the mysterious cultists, or were the craft really UFOs? In northern England, where cases of slaughtered sheep were being attributed to ghostly wild cats, and without any knowledge of comparable sightings in the USA, the 'phantom helicopter', as the police dubbed it, was regularly seen hopping low across the hills late at night.

The attacks continued over the years. In May 1973, as more reports of mutilations were received, two women driving near Houston, Texas, observed a bright light in the sky. Under hypnotic regression conducted by psychologist Dr Leo Sprinkle, they told of seeing a cow being sucked up into a giant craft and then being taken aboard themselves. Here they watched helpless as aliens dissected parts of the animal and conducted an experiment.

In January 1978, again in northern England, ironically by the Devil's Garden, beside the River Weaver at Frodsham, Cheshire, several poachers claimed to have seen a silver bell-like object land. Some strange beings with 'miners' lamps' on their head emerged and placed a frame or cage around a paralysed cow as if they were taking measurements of its body.

Linda Moulton Howe, an American researcher and TV producer, won an EMMY award for her documentary *A Strange Harvest*, putting together the US mutilation evidence for the first time. She has continued her work and reports a major wave of mutilated cows in mid-western states during the summer of 1992. Although these remain unexplained, she seems convinced that they are directly related to alien spacenapping cases.

A detailed investigation by sceptics, published soon after Howe's documentary, reached quite the opposite conclusion, effectively arguing that there were no more than the usual number of dead cows being discovered and that these could all have

mundane causes. Predators were blamed for the alleged mutilations after death.

The destructive report *Mute Evidence*, by Daniel Kagan and Ian Summers, split the research community. Some accepted their findings as an indication that it constitutes, as Jerome Clark termed it in 1993, 'one of the most durable myths of the late twentieth century'. Others are not so satisfied that the mystery is over. As long as cows apparently drained of blood continue to be found on American ranches, this viewpoint is unlikely to be changed.

1967 20 OCTOBER

BIGFOOT FILM

The most impressive and controversial evidence for the reality of 'Bigfoot' was reputedly captured just after 1 p.m. on this day by Roger Patterson and Bob Gimlin. They were riding in the Six Rivers Forest of northern California when they had a close observation of a large unidentified figure.

Roger Patterson's cine-film sequence of Bigfoot, claimed to be the American counterpart of the Asiatic Yeti.

Right: Nazca lines in the Peruvian desert, claimed by Erich von Däniken to be the work of ancient astronauts.
Above: Nazca sand drawings of 'spacemen', a fish and an unidentified animal.

By the mid-1970s the ancient astronauts furore had largely died down, lacking, as it did, the resilience of other widely criticized theories, such as the concept of the Bermuda Triangle. Yet it undoubtedly generated interesting speculations and provoked an examination of myths and legends from other cultures where there does indeed seem to be a broadly similar pattern to stories about 'gods' descending in 'fiery chariots' from the skies before recorded history began.

Von Däniken still continues his work, well tempered by criticism. In 1991 he wrote the foreword to a German translation of a cautiously objective book that I co-authored, which many will see as a positive step.

1972 29 DECEMBER

AIRLINE APPARITION

One of the most remarkable hauntings of all time began with the crash of an Eastern Airlines L-1011 Tristar aircraft as it headed into Miami Airport above the Florida Everglades – a network of alligator-infested shallow river swamps.

Flight 401 had come from New York with 176 people aboard, which in itself was noteworthy: it should have had well over 200 passengers but an unusually large number of them cancelled for unknown reasons at the last minute. Did they have a premonition of disaster?

One of the stewardesses certainly did. She told colleagues of seeing the plane come down on flat watery land. But she was spared the struggle with her conscience – and perhaps her life was saved – by being switched to another route shortly beforehand.

All aircraft instrumentation failed three hours after takeoff. With the unlit terrain below offering no visual clues, the wide-bodied jet flew straight into the ground instead of on to the runway. Despite a massive impact, splintering the hull into pieces, the damp conditions prevented a fire and more than one-third of those on board had a miraculous escape.

Not so lucky were pilot Bob Loft and second officer Don Repo. However, in the following months and years doubts grew among Eastern Airlines staff as to whether they really had died. Repo's presence, in particular, was felt aboard several other Tristars in the fleet, especially those using parts salvaged from the wrecked jet.

Crews reported experiencing sudden temperature drops, strange sensations and even images of Repo himself reflected in the shiny surface of equipment. Many stewardesses confirmed such things to researcher John Fuller.

The most intriguing story came from a pilot who did not know Repo. He was warned of a fire risk by a man in the spare seat sitting next to him. Assuming him to be an airline engineer taking the flight, he checked the suggested circuits. There was a fault and probable disaster was averted. When the captain turned to offer thanks, the mysterious engineer had vanished. From descriptions, other crew members recognized the man as Don Repo.

In 1973 Repo's ghost reportedly told the crew that 'they' (he and Bob Loft?) would never allow another L-1011 to crash. Indeed, Eastern's large fleet of forty-nine jets continued to have an impressive and unblemished record. Moreover, no other L-1011 of any airline crashed for more than a decade.

The promise appeared to have ended on 2 August 1985 when a Delta Airways Tristar was hit by awesome wind sheer during a fierce storm as it landed at Dallas Airport. It was smashed against the runway. Yet even here, despite the incredible inferno and carnage that resulted, thirty-one people walked out of the wreckage, which many experts considered a virtual miracle. Perhaps they had some unseen help from beyond the grave?

1973

BEND! BEND! BEND!

The most dramatic new phenomenon of the early 1970s was undoubtedly the appearance of Israeli psychic Uri Geller. Although he had been using what he claimed were great powers to perform in his native land for several years, it was in 1973 that he came to the world's attention.

Several researchers in California, including Dr Jacques Vallee, tested his reputed abilities by conducting experiments at the Stanford Institute. They used ESP and newly developed 'remote viewing' techniques, whereby Geller was asked to draw a sketch that an out-of-view 'sitter' had pro-

Above: image beamed to England from Africa by the author in one of Uri Geller's remote-viewing experiments.
Below: Geller demonstrates his paranormal powers on TV.

duced, or to detect information about a remote location by tuning in and mentally seeing through the eyes of the person who had gone there.

After these tests in the USA, Geller came to Britain and became an instant TV celebrity thanks to one of his 'party tricks', which was never his main claim to fame. This was his apparent ability to cause metal objects such as spoons and keys to warp in front of the eyes of an audience, expert scientists such as Dr Lyall Watson and even TV cameras beaming the effect to millions. As a result of his focusing hard, sometimes repeating words such as 'Bend!', and stroking it lightly with his fingers, the spoon did indeed seem to do exactly that.

Geller was a smash hit, but immediately enraged the sceptics – who enlisted great support from professional magicians. They argued that this was a simple trick and demonstrated several methods by which it could be done. They spoke of using an acid to weaken the stem of the spoon (although tests showed this was not employed by Geller) or how by sleight of hand he could distract the watching millions, give a malleable spoon a quick jerk and then release it from his palms apparently as if bent by magic. When Geller succeeded with objects such as heavy keys that could only be twisted within a vice, he was accused of pre-bending replicas. They would not accept that he could be genuine.

Clearly the magicians felt he was cheating their profession by winning undeserved fame through an evidently spurious claim to be a psychic. They waged a long and bitter war that never abated. In 1992 Geller and James 'the Amazing' Randi (an American magician and fervent psychic debunker) even fought it out in the courtroom. Randi quit his position with CSICOP (Committee Investigating Claims of the Paranormal), formed during the 1970s to defend science against mysticism, in the event they were brought into the matter. Geller won initial legal rounds, but at time of writing the cases are ongoing and the debate seems certain to continue.

Whatever the truth about this undoubtedly amiable showman, his spoon-bending created a wave of imitators in the 1970s, particularly among British children. Suddenly everyone was doing it! The scientific experiments that were set up to test these wonder kids had the beneficial effect of arousing the interest of physical scientists who had begun to write off parapsychology as difficult to test and more properly the province of soft sciences such as psychology and sociology.

Sadly, Geller did himself few favours within the community of serious paranormal research, where he had received wide support, by resorting to some odd byways. These included taking photographs of bloblike UFOs through an aircraft window and associating with a group that claimed contact with a group of ethereal beings known as 'The Nine', led by a force called 'Hoova'.

Nevertheless, Uri Geller had the last laugh on everyone. Between the late 1970s and late 1980s he 'disappeared', to emerge a very wealthy man. He boasted that he had used the talents disputed by so many sceptics to help big corporations locate rich mineral deposits. Spoon-bending, with which he is still closely associated, was never more than a sideshow to his real talents.

1975 8 AUGUST

BALL LIGHTNING

Possibly the best documented case of this still puzzling natural phenomenon occurred in England, when a woman, cooking in her kitchen during a thunderstorm, observed a blue/purple globe of light, about the size of a tennis ball and surrounded by a fiery ring, right above the cooker. Then it flew directly at her, striking her below the stomach with a rattling noise and giving off a smell of burning. She felt a heat sensation and found a hole through her clothes but was not seriously hurt. However, the hand with which she had tried to bat the ball away swelled up, becoming red and inflamed, and the skin underneath her wedding ring was scalded.

A spectacular shot of ball lightning, taken in Austria in summer 1978.

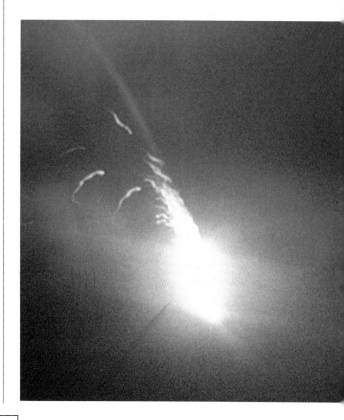

Given so much physical evidence to study in this case, even formerly sceptical scientists had to accept the reality of the phenomenon (which may occur in calm conditions as well as during storms, either indoors or outdoors). A topic that for many years had been considered paranormal became a part of mainstream science, debated in journals such as *Nature*.

Remarkably, many of the effects described, like the wedding ring effect, have also featured in UFO close encounters and seem to be caused by 'eddy currents' circulating in the metal ring. Researchers such as Dr Paul Davies, a physicist at Adelaide University, believe that it could be worth exploring the possibility of an energy cross-over between such phenomena.

Paranormal researchers often point to ball lightning as a still unsolved mystery that has recently made the transition from myth to scientific reality, confident that it may be followed by others in the future.

 **1975** 18 DECEMBER

THE AMITYVILLE HAUNTING

Possibly the most famous case of a haunting began on this day when George and Kathy Lutz moved into their imposing new house on Ocean Avenue in the suburb of Amityville on Long Island, New York. They had bought it cheaply, because thirteen months previously a man had murdered six people in their beds while living in the building.

What happened in the four weeks before the Lutz family allegedly fled in terror provoked a best-selling book – Jay Anson's *The Amityville Horror* (1978), a movie and a string of sequels that continue to appear in the 1990s, although by now bearing little, if any, relationship to events that occurred in the house in December 1975.

According to the story told by the Lutz family, as narrated in Anson's book, almost every recorded incident from poltergeist outbreaks and past hauntings were crammed into this one single case. They included oozing slime in the bathroom, horrible smells pervading rooms, invisible forces grabbing hold of family members and heavy objects moving around of their own volition. Even when the Lutz family departed – unusually in such cases – they claimed that the evil force pursued them to their next home.

A number of independent investigations by paranormal researchers found it impossible to verify much of the story. Police denied any involvement. The priest who supposedly 'blessed' the house said he never went inside. No local workers could recall repairing the alleged damage to the building caused by the wrecking force. Although few doubted that the family did believe that something had happened to them, their original reports (prior to the book and the movie) were less dramatic, referring to feelings and sensations rather than to anything very physical or substantial.

It later emerged that the defence lawyer for the previous occupant had recognized that his attempts to fathom the reasons for the latter's crime might benefit from the belief in a terrible evil within the house, coupled with his client's claims of a voice possessing his mind. Other factors probably contributed to the escalation of the story as it progressed.

Whereas it is difficult to determine the absolute truth in this case, it seems unlikely that the incidents were any more dramatic than dozens of other hauntings that have been described by terrified individuals and families throughout this century. This one, however, was expertly promoted.

RETURN FROM DEATH

In 1975, an American psychiatrist, Dr Raymond Moody, published his extraordinary book *Life After Life*, which became a bestseller. Although the phenomenon in question was not new, the book popularized the subject for the first time and, by offering positive hope of life after death, struck a responsive chord.

As Moody noted, people had for centuries occasionally returned from the brink of death to claim they had seen a bright light, at the end of which they had met deceased friends or relatives. Whether they had been to heaven and back or had merely been hallucinating depended on one's religious viewpoint.

Moody simply collected a group of stories and showed that this phenomenon was happening more and more in a world of medical miracles where revival from massive heart attacks and recovery from once-fatal coma were becoming routine. More importantly, however, he defined a common pattern for such cases, some of which exhibited many of the features he described.

In the archetypal example of what came to be called the near death experience (NDE), people first report finding themselves floating above the body and free of any pain they might have been suffering as a result of a car crash, surgical operation or the like. This was by far the most common aspect of the NDE and had long been recognized by paranormal researchers as an out-of-body experience (OOBE).

Following the OOBE, some of Moody's patients had reported seeing a bright light, being sucked toward it along a tube or tunnel, having a feeling of peace and tranquillity, and (in very rare cases) seeing figures, such as dead relatives or a godlike being. They might enter a beautiful environment, such as a garden of rich and harmonious colours, and then make a rational decision to return home, often to protect their family. As a result they would zip back into their previous state of pain and suffering, to discover a medical team fighting to save their life.

Of course, it was soon appreciated that these people had not died, only been near

to death, hence the term that was applied to the phenomenon. But it was very tempting to think that the experience provided solid, repeatable data about an afterlife, brought to the fore by scientific progress.

Many other researchers began to do tests that were much more systematic, and various research associations were launched. The paranormal community was fascinated, seeking parallels with other forms of experience. It was quickly realized that there were definite links, for example, with alleged reports of spacenapping – in which witnesses entered an OOBE after being struck by a tubelike beam and then found themselves in a strange environment, surrounded by more intelligent, usually humanoid but dimly perceived beings. Perhaps only the interpretation was different here.

The significant point was that mainstream researchers, too, were intrigued by NDE. It was a paranormal subject that attracted attention well beyond the realms of the supernatural.

A University of Connecticut psychologist, Dr Kenneth Ring, began to study such cases and eventually saw the links with alien abductions. His books mark the transition of his work across a fourteen-year period.

A medical specialist in heart trauma, Dr Michael Sabom, collected data from his patients, expecting to disprove the reality of NDEs. He was forced in the other direction, checking the details of the revival techniques these people actually saw while floating above the casualty room in a hospital. Whereas some had only a superficial, often simplified and misleading, concept of the methods employed, based perhaps on TV dramas, NDE victims were able to give astonishingly detailed accounts of how they were saved from death by medical expertise.

NDE research gradually attracted even more specialists. One of the more recent is Dr Melvin Morse, from Seattle, Washington, who has focused on NDEs reported by young

Representations of the out-of-body experience. Is it proof of an afterlife or simply hallucination?

children. Like his colleagues, he, too, has noticed that the overwhelming majority of patients emerge from an NDE with no fear of death. Indeed, they believe the process they have experienced to be pleasant. Morse had one young patient who said of an NDE, 'I am not afraid to go back to that place.' Shortly afterwards he had another attack from which he did not recover.

Sceptics, of course, rebelled. Early notions about hallucinations triggered by administered drugs faltered largely because NDEs also occurred in accident situations long before – or in total absence of – any medical aid. Theories about visions caused by inoxia (starvation of oxygen to the brain as death approaches) seemed more plausible, but Sabom measured this in his cases and was able to show an NDE where inoxia was considered impossible.

In 1992, Dr Sue Blackmore, a psychologist at the University of Western England, who was initially a pro-OOBE researcher but gradually became convinced that these were complex hallucinations, produced her 'dying brain' theory for NDEs. This involved a series of phenomena, from randomly firing optic nerves, shown by computer simulation to form a tunnel image, to natural chemicals (called endorphins) produced by the body to deaden pain and induce euphoria. Another critical finding was that NDEs also occur in cases where physical death is never likely (e.g. an almost unharmed mountaineer falling into soft snow). Why would he then have a 'near death' experience? The debate rages on.

1977

ONE WEEK IN MAY

By the late 1970s we knew a great deal more about how the paranormal worked than ever before. The new hard-headed approach had paid dividends and researchers were looking beyond the

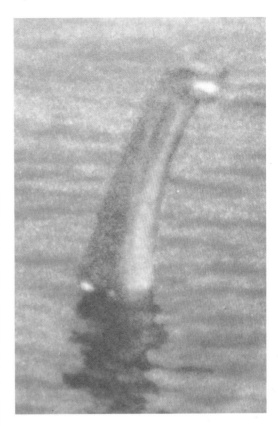

'Doc' Shiels took his controversial photograph of Nessie amidst a wave of strange events throughout Britain.

extreme divide of 'it's either this or it must be that' (usually the most exotic possible solution or a complete nonsense) to arrive at more balanced positions. Terms such as 'middle UFOlogy' were even being used by UFO researchers who were persuaded that real things were happening that science did not yet understand, but were unwilling to accept that aliens riding spaceships were the only alternatives to mass hallucination.

Two major clues to emerge were, first, that various paranormal phenomena occurred in sudden, intense periods of activity and then went quiet for a time before flaring up again, and second, that there were localized focal points where activity occurred far more often than chance might dictate. French researcher Fernand Lagarde had also spotted the link between these zones and heavy fault lines in rocks beneath the Earth's surface. Both these ideas were given a big boost in May 1977 when Britain was hit by its most dramatic burst of strange phenomena ever squeezed into a single week.

During the third week of the month all manner of things were let loose in what is variously termed a 'flap', when of short duration, or a 'wave', when spread over several weeks. The most active locations during such periods are those focal points known as 'windows', which were gradually being isolated.

There were more UFO sightings in Britain than in any other year, before or since. That single week in May generated almost 10 per cent of that total. These were usually little more than lights in the sky darting about the landscape, but the numbers (well over seventy cases) were phenomenal.

However, other amazing things went on as well. Centres of poltergeist activity, with apparitions, strange noises and weird energies, burst into sudden life. The phantom big cats were again loose in moorland areas. And in Loch Ness, on 21 May, the most astounding photographs ever taken were claimed by 'Doc' Shiels, a magician and showman who was said to 'evoke' monsters into life. Argument still rages over his full-colour shots of the neck and open mouth of Nessie, particularly given their semi-transparent feel.

Whatever the truth, forces seem to have been at work between 17 and 25 May that set many different experiences in motion. There were even crop circles found in English fields, although no such phenomenon had yet been recognized, so that examples mostly went unnoticed.

Periods like this showed an interesting comparison with solar flare activity, which could cause disruption (e.g. by interfering with telecommunications) when charged particles reached the Earth. The Sun might then go quiet again until the next burst of intense activity.

Researchers such as Paul Devereux and others, particularly in Britain and France, were developing the idea that certain 'windows' were periodically set into motion, perhaps also producing charged particles that floated freely into the air and as a result created strange phenomena in the atmosphere. But what made an area into a window and what factors caused it to flare up as it had in May 1977?

As if on cue, two Canadian researchers at Laurentian University, Ontario, neurophysiologist Dr Michael Persinger and his assistant Ghyslaine Lafreniere, published a massive study of computer data. They had examined thousands of reports of mysterious phenomena in an attempt to isolate a common pattern. They proposed that electrical columns of energy (which they called 'transients') could be produced at certain places and during certain periods, and that these might be perceived as glowing forms when they illuminated the gases in the air. Because of their high energy output, they could even scramble the neural pathways in the brain of anyone coming too close. The result of this could be a subjective mental experience, the origin of which depended upon a novel energy phenomenon that science had yet to identify but which was actually present. These things were not simply hallucinations.

This bridge between physical reality and subjective vision was accepted enthusiastically by some European researchers who quickly recognized its potential to account for the sort of activity that had occurred during May 1977.

1977 27 OCTOBER

CONTACT WITH THE SPIRIT WORLD

If George Meek is to be believed, this was one of the most important dates in human history. Using a series of modifications and improvements on the EVP tape-recorder experiments from the 1960s, he announced that his 'Spiricom' device had forged two-way contact with the spirit world.

Meek, a wealthy American inventor, with the assistance of a trained psychic, had produced robotic sounds that reputedly came from two scientists in the afterlife calling themelves 'Doc Nick' and 'Dr Mueller'. Mueller was traced, together with some fairly obscure material that he published before his death and which matched a quotation that he gave through Spiricom. These ethereal co-workers also proposed ways to improve the equipment before Mueller had to 'move on' in the spirit world and thus passed out of contact.

Those who have studied Spiricom seem impressed by the device, which has been made available to other researchers. However, there are some qualms about the banality of conversations and the way modern idioms are used by the occasional stray voices that intrude and yet profess to have died up to 150 years ago.

Sceptics also point out that the voices greatly resemble those that emerge from an artificial larynx, as used by victims of throat cancer. Tests have suggested, nevertheless, that there are two separate voices on the

Bent and twisted rock layers in the Canary Islands, one of the world's major 'window areas'.

The author investigating a 'window area' in the Pennine Hills of Yorkshire. Strange lights and noises as well as electrical poltergeist attacks have been reported from this isolated location.

tapes and that the psychic operator is not simply throwing his own voice in the manner of a ventriloquist.

George Meek has no doubts. This, he says, is absolute proof of survival of bodily death. Indeed, since Spiricom, the team has attempted to turn this radio link to heaven into a TV set tuned to the same frequency.

1978 21 OCTOBER

THE VANISHING CESSNA

Frederick Valentich was the 20-year-old pilot of a rented Cessna 182 aircraft. He took off in the early evening to fly the short hop across the Bass Straits from Melbourne to King Island, midway between the Australian mainland and Tasmania. His mission was to collect some shellfish for friends

but he was never to be seen again.

The disappearance, far from being unremarked, was one of the strangest on record. The whole sequence of events was picked up and taped from the ground-to-air radio communications with the airport control tower; yet, despite such extraordinary evidence, the lengthy investigation still failed to resolve what had happened to this man.

Valentich, fairly inexperienced in flying over water at night, reported seeing odd lights which were travelling above him as if keeping watch. The conversation became more strained as he alleged that his engine was suffering problems while the lights on a large, dark craft (which he confirmed was 'hovering' and 'not an aircraft') flew alongside. Then there was a strange grinding noise on the microphone – and silence.

Countless theories were proposed. One was that he had been hit by a meteor. Another suggested that he ran foul of drug smugglers who flew a helicopter above him and used nets to trail their catch home in the water below – the unfortunate Cessna becoming entangled with these in mid-flight. Dr Richard Haines, an American specialist in the aviation field, did extensive work and speculated that a secret laser experiment from an American intelligence base called Pine Gap might have been involved and somehow gone wrong.

The most widely debated theory, however, was that the lights described by Valentich belonged to a UFO. Indeed there was an ongoing 'flap' over the Bass Strait area at the time. Was Valentich spacenapped along with his plane? One abductee in the USA has since claimed that the aliens have confirmed this as 'fact' and that the young man remains healthy – on another planet!

The theory advanced by most sceptics is that the pilot engineered his own disappearance. They point to his interest in UFOs (he had a scrapbook of stories with him on the flight) and also to the fact that he appears deliberately to have delayed his departure at the last minute until it was dark. He also took with him several times too much fuel for the journey.

However, if this is so, why did Valentich hatch such an elaborate plan and what happened to the Cessna aircraft? His family do not accept the theory and the truth is that we shall probably never know.

1979 26 MAY

THE CINCINNATI PREMONITION

Possibly the most remarkable case of precognition ever reported concerns a 23-year-old office manager named David Booth from Cincinnati, Ohio. For ten days prior to this date he had had the same dream, seeing a certain plane crash in flames into an area full of buildings.

On 22 May he was so troubled by his vivid experience that he called the Federal Aviation Authority and also spoke with American Airlines, as identified in his vision. In desperation he also talked to a psychiatrist who specialized in dreams.

Booth was never in doubt that his experience was a premonition. He said that he saw, heard and felt the entire thing again and again. It was like watching it unfold on a TV or cinema screen, far clearer than a normal dream.

Soon convinced that Booth was neither a crank nor a practical joker, the Aviation Authority did what it could. It tried to link his account with an aircraft type and an airport – assuming, as did Booth, that Cincinnati was the most likely candidate. However, as the authority pointed out, it could not ground every American Airlines flight indefinitely, even from a single airport.

On 26 May the final dream occurred. Meanwhile, at Chicago's O'Hare Airport, TV actress Lindsay Wagner (famous for her role as the 'Bionic Woman' with special powers) was due to board an American Airlines flight with her mother. But she was overcome with a sick feeling and could not leave. She cancelled their reservations and the DC-10 jet took off without them. Seconds after it cleared the runway, an engine fell off and the plane crashed into an horrific fireball near buildings at the edge of the airport. Everyone on board was killed instantly.

After the accident a spokesman for the Civil Aviation Authority confirmed that many details of the crash matched the dreams that Booth had reported both to them and to the airline operating the doomed plane. They could easily match up airline, aircraft type and airport from his descriptions after the fatal incident, but how could they possibly have prevented catastrophe?

David Booth himself has never understood why he was given this incredible preview of such a terrible event, culminating in what proved a futile attempt to change the future. He had no direct link with the aircraft or its passengers. The events merely left him scarred emotionally by a terrible disaster that he had been powerless to prevent.

113

SOCIETY AND THE UNEXPLAINED

The possibility of global warfare receded but was replaced by new horrors. The disease AIDS became recognized as a worldwide plague which had a fundamental effect on people's morals and long-term perspectives. Scientists found a hole growing in the ozone layer—a protective covering that if stripped away could have devastating effects for all future life; and harmful gases in the atmosphere threatened to produce a 'greenhouse effect', with possible dire consequences for the Earth's climate.

The need to preserve and perhaps save our planet was reflected in paranormal phenomena. Even the aliens offered a 'green message' as UFO sightings declined in number. The world was turning away from outer space to look more closely at the inner space reality.

1980 1989

1980

CIRCULAR SIGNS

In August 1980 a farmer found two flattened areas etched into his crop of oats in a field at Westbury, Wiltshire, in southern England. They had straight edges and were about 60 feet in diameter. He had come across one earlier in the summer and assumed it to be a weather effect. Now he was not so sure. Before harvesting, he reported it and a UFO group from Bristol came out to have a closer look at the phenomenon.

This group, Probe, was one of the new breed of serious researchers and did not assume that the circles were landing pads of a spaceship. After simple tests failed to establish anything supernatural, the investigators consulted a local meteorologist, Dr Terence Meaden, who thought it likely that some kind of rotating vortex, such as a whirlwind, was the cause of the mysterious patterns.

The matter achieved brief notoriety when another UFOlogist did suggest the spacecraft option to a news source, but in truth the subject failed to inspire many people that summer.

In 1981 and 1982, only isolated circles were found. Then, in 1983, eight appeared across southern England and in a strange formation: a central circle surrounded by four satellites. This shape, much more consistent with the landing legs of a spacecraft, was a blow to Dr Meaden, Probe and their supporters, who for three years had provided persuasive reports that these simple circles were natural and weather-induced. Although Terence Meaden tried to incorporate the new design (and the ever more elaborate ones that appeared in the follow-

The hole in the centre of this swirled patch of crop betrays the likelihood of a hoaxed circle.

A variety of crop circles: many of the more elaborate formations have proved to be faked.

ing years), he was losing the battle as these complex marks came to bear the all too clear signs of artificiality. This was welcome news to the sceptics.

A UFOlogist named Pat Delgado, joined in 1985 by Colin Andrews, began to document reports in the journal *Flying Saucer Review*, and the photographs (often taken by private pilot 'Busty' Taylor) proved captivating. Delgado also went out of his way to involve the media. The tabloids were not slow to use the spaceship landings theory as a silly season filler story. After much attention in July 1983, it was resurrected almost every summer, with whatever new angle emerged.

The first hoaxed circle (by a national newspaper!) was exposed during 1983. Given the publicity, more were clearly happening. Despite the claims of experts, nobody could reliably distinguish real from fake.

Meaden enjoyed strong support from serious UFOlogists for his 'weather plus hoaxing' idea (although it was a while before hoaxing was perceived as more than a minor irritation). A few researchers, like Delgado, believed an 'unknown intelligence' (definitely not human) was at work. Because the media saw mileage in this idea, but not in the more sober weather theory, it received undue publicity. It all helped to sustain interest.

Whereas 90 per cent of all circles (hundreds of which were appearing all over the world by the late 1980s) were simple, single patterns, as the very first ones had been, the media concentrated instead on the comparatively few outrageous (and, as we now know, certainly hoaxed) formations. These were spectacular and were duly named pictograms, to imply that they were

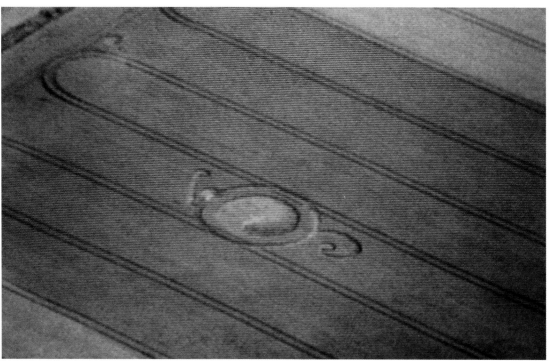

a form of message or communication from an alien presence. But they were far fewer in number than the publicity afforded to them must have implied.

Attempts to decode their message soon involved the environmental fringe and before long ideas surfaced that the Earth's 'soul' was sending a plea for help or that the 'spirit world' was giving visible evidence of dangers to the food chain if we did not mend our ways. Gurus such as David Icke, who left his job as a TV presenter to embark on an esoteric spiritual crusade, entered the fray. This, of course, reinforced media attention, as did countless competitions and best-selling books by the cereologists (as members of the movement now called themselves).

The original researchers — Meaden and his UFOlogical colleagues — fought hard to bring reason to bear, pointing out that simple circles had been known for centuries and quoting examples back to the year 1590. They also traced dozens of eyewitnesses to the later versions, who described no aliens but instead what appeared to be the presence of a rotating air vortex. There were also experiments in wind tunnels, computer simulations and other forms of enquiry in universities (especially in Japan and the USA) that established hard evidence of a so-called plasma vortex — an electrified, rotating air column which could glow as it spun to Earth and which, in fact, bears more than a passing similarity to Persinger's 'transients', as first proposed in 1977.

Yet, in spite of the books packed with hard evidence, the serious articles in highbrow newspapers and a few pieces in the scientific press, the popularity of the cereology movement was hardly dented. The latter offered little solid evidence and speculated widely about strange powers at work, guided by unseen and unknown intelligences. It was this idea, however, that people wanted to believe, and the tourists flooded in.

1980 6 JANUARY

FIRE TRAGEDY

An extraordinary case of spontaneous human combustion (SHC) was discovered by police and forensic officers in a living-room at Blackwood, Ebbw Vale, in Wales. The male occupant was almost totally consumed by the localized fire that had barely damaged an armchair in which he sat and had failed to melt nearby plastic objects. Yet the heat had been of such intensity as to leave a coating of vaporized flesh on the ceiling.

This was just one of a series of incidents in 1980. Ten per cent of all known cases of SHC took place during this year for reasons that are still unexplained.

1980 29 DECEMBER

ATTACK FROM THE AIR

Although UFO incidents were by now on the decrease, when they did occur they could be of epic proportions. Two extraordinary events, took place almost simultaneously on either side of the Atlantic Ocean.

The first spanned several nights between 26 and 29 December and involved American airmen from the twin English NATO bases of Woodbridge and Bentwaters in Suffolk. Civilians travelling along a forested road and in nearby scattered villages and farming communities also saw the giant lights crashing from the sky.

A hole was left in the pine-tree canopy, three indentations were traced in the ground and twice the normal background count of radiation was measured in the area some twenty-four hours later. A security patrol sent into Rendlesham Forest on the perimeter of the bases described a conical object, the size of a car, which outpaced them as it gave chase. Several witnesses describe losing periods of time and seeing small creatures close by.

In the course of measuring the traces in the early hours of the second night, a return encounter with UFOs was tape-recorded 'live' — a copy of which eventually reached UFOlogists in 1984. A British RAF radar base had allegedly tracked the object on the previous night heading into East Anglia.

Because of limited information release after two years of denials by the British Ministry of Defence, a lot of confusion still surrounds this case.

However, the memorandum filed with the British government by the deputy base commander, Colonel Charles Halt, was squeezed out in 1983 under the American Freedom of Information Act. This confirmed some of the evidence, including Halt's own sighting of unexplained lights. Other data, such as the photographs which are clearly referenced on the tape-recording as they are taken, remain withheld, as do any results of the military investigations that must have resulted.

On 29 December, a night when more lights were seen in Rendlesham Forest, another military incident unfolded more than 3000 miles away at Huffman, near Houston, Texas. Three people in a car (two women and their young grandson) claim to have seen a glowing object not unlike that witnessed by the airmen in the English forest. However, it was being shepherded by several military helicopters, as if heading toward a base. The presence of these earthly craft has consistently been denied by the US government.

The three witnesses felt tremendous heat pouring from the object and all became ill, suffering from nausea, blisters, rashes and eye problems, suggesting exposure to radiation. One of the women, who had stood outside the car in front of the conical object, spent several weeks in hospital and was for a time critically ill from what

Sketch of the object seen by US airmen at the Bentwaters base in their close encounter experience.

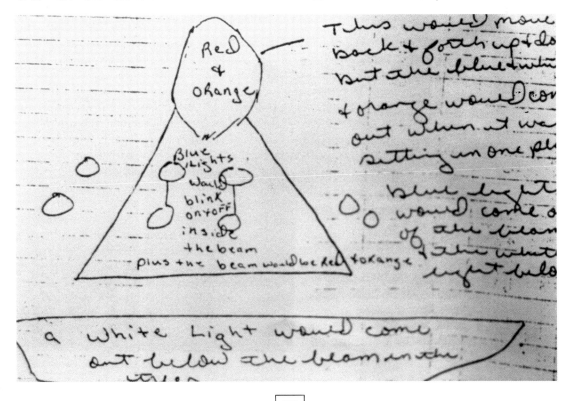

SOCIETY AND THE UNEXPLAINED

An impression by Roy Sandbach of a mysterious ball of light stalling a car engine.

appears to have been radiation sickness. Huge clumps of her hair fell out before she gradually recovered.

The victims sued the US government for their considerable medical expenses on the grounds that if this was not a secret weapon of the USA (as was insisted), the military had the responsibility to protect them, regardless of origin. The costs involved in fighting the case became prohibitive after their initial arguments were stonewalled.

1981

THE HESSDALEN LIGHTS

Late in this year people in the mountainous area of Hessdalen, a remote valley north of Trondheim in Norway, began to see strange glows in the sky. They were not connected with the aurora that was commonly observed here. These were free-floating masses of energy drifting through the air and low across mountaintops. They appeared sporadically, particularly during December and January, in succeeding years.

In 1984 and 1985, a team of UFO experts calling themselves 'Project Hessdalen' made the trek, with temperatures far below zero, into the snowbound region. They had gathered together a caravan and expensive equipment, including radar and lasers, as well as sophisticated cameras and meters to record radiation emissions. They were partly funded by the UFO community around Europe but they also received temporary loans from scientific establishments and unexpected help from the Scandinavian defence authorities who had alerted aircraft when sightings were being reported.

The several weeks spent in these expeditions were highly rewarding. This was clearly a window area that was unusually active at the time, and with such powerful equipment to measure and record it, the team were almost guaranteed to make a breakthrough.

Of course, the researchers saw plenty of IFOs (stars, aircraft and other identified flying objects). But they also recorded several impressive glowing lights, usually red or blue in colour. Not only did they take excellent photographs but they obtained other readings of the structure of these phenomena. With the addition of later research by meteorologists, this suggested that they were witnessing what might be a type of atmospheric plasma somehow generated in the area and whose origin was unknown. The sum total of written and visual evidence was truly impressive.

One type of UFO had finally been snared simply by the combined efforts of rational enthusiasts and scientists who were for once unafraid to face the possibility of finding something strange.

A strange glowing light above the Hessdalen valley in Norway, later the subject of intensive scientific study.

1982

THE EARTH IS ALIVE

For some years researchers had worked on similar tracks, slowly converging upon one another. Lagarde in France had found a link between UFOs and fault lines below the Earth's surface. Persinger had defined a transient as an electrical force in the air at prime locations, which created windows that focused all sorts of strange activity. Studies of a window area in the Pennine Hills of England had led to the belief that natural energy forms called UAP (unidentified atmospheric phenomena) were at work. And Dr Meaden had come up with a plasma vortex to explain genuine crop circles.

Paul Devereux was a researcher into Earth mysteries. During the early 1980s, particular attention was being paid to sites such as Avebury and Stonehenge and hundreds of other lesser known stone circles throughout northern Europe. Thousands of years ago, people set in place standing stones, for reasons that remain obscure. Yet scientists working on the rocks were finding

Stonehenge, Wiltshire, may be a focal point for the glowing bursts of energy known as 'earthlights'.

bursts of energy being emitted, especially at sunrise and sunset, as if the stones were channelling some force from the ground.

Devereux combined much of this work to describe an energy trapped within the body of the Earth itself and which could be released into the atmosphere by some mechanism as yet undetermined. It would focus at window areas and could provoke various strange phenomena when unleashed, from poltergeist attacks to mysterious explosions and buzzing noises. He also felt that these could create chemical reactions by exciting gases in the atmosphere, producing a glowing effect like a plasma. He invented the term 'earthlight' for these effects and his 1982 book defined its parameters.

Although Devereux was talking about the same types of phenomena that many others were approaching from different directions, he went one step further. He suggested that the energy was interactive with the consciousness of those who experienced it, and that perhaps they were able to affect its shape and manner of formation. Since quantum physics was indicating that consciousness might well be a coordinating force at the sub-atomic level of reality, this idea was not as wild as once it might have seemed. Interestingly, researchers at the Hessdalen window later noted how some of the phenomena that they recorded seemed to respond to their laser beam emissions as if they were interacting with the thoughts of the experimenters.

The concept of earthlights, vortices, plasmas and transients being activated at window areas around the world and generating energy fields that could explain a range of paranormal phenomena was viewed in Europe as an exciting breakthrough. However, in other countries, notably the USA, paranormal researchers were far less tolerant. It remains a fringe theory in many respects and the desire to find more exotic explanations is promoted by the tabloid media, who perceive such things as earthlights either as sceptical debunking or spoilsport tactics. For scientists it still remains too strange for automatic acceptance. As such, this work still lacks the support it needs to establish itself as either science or parascience.

1982 OCTOBER

PSYCHIC QUESTING

The publication of the book *The Green Stone* by Graham Phillips and Martin Keatman established a new kind of supernatural event by reporting on the first in a line of 'psychic quests'. This had apparently arisen unexpectedly during recent years when a group of psychics began to receive interlocking messages. Individually these meant little, but when brought together by Keatman, Phillips and colleague Andy Collins, who then ran an esoteric magazine entitled *Strange Phenomena*, they seemed to make sense.

The saga that eventually unfolded was like a cross between the quest for the Holy Grail and a version of Tolkien's *Lord of the Rings*. There were intriguing parallels, too, with *The Chronicles of Thomas Covenant* by Stephen Donaldson, a series of hugely successful fantasy novels then being published.

The British psychics, together with researchers and witnesses to strange phenomena, found themselves dragged into a search for a sword buried in the foundations of an old bridge, and then, using the sword to interpret the visions, to the discovery of a small green stone that had to be charged with energy at Earth mystery sites such as the Avebury stone circle. The purpose of all this effort was apparently to protect the Earth against a malevolent force that was trying to seize control — a task that had previously been assigned to the owners of those same artefacts after they had arrived in Britain from Egypt following the reign of the pharaoh Akhenaten.

The story reads like a typical 'dungeons and dragons' — a role-play fantasy game popular in the Eighties. However, the many people involved in the quest swear to its truth. They engaged in real 'psychic battles' and experienced countless strange phenomena as they lived through the affair.

Psychic quests centred on the discovery of swords claimed to interpret supernatural visions.

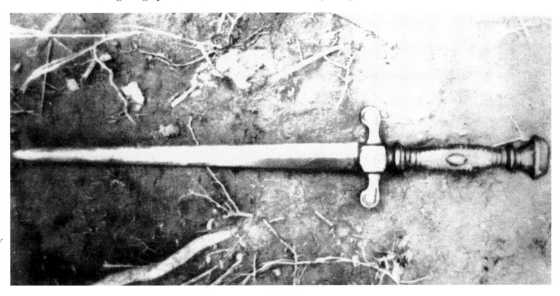

Several further quests followed, in which six other swords and various coloured stones were discovered. A battle was allegedly fought with an evil force which unleashed the unforeseen killer hurricane on southern Britain in October 1987.

Andy Collins has written eloquently and entertainingly of the later quests for an eager readership, seemingly entranced by this strange (and so far uniquely British) modern mystery.

Avebury, Wiltshire, is associated with energy emissions investigated by psychics.

1985

ESP-IONAGE

Reports began to surface that the CIA and KGB were fighting a 'war' on the basis of information (termed PSI) obtained from psychics.

It had been known for some years that the Soviet Union had funded much research into paranormal phenomena. There were strong rumours of a successful telepathy experiment carried out between ground control and a Russian spaceflight while in orbit. Western visitors to Soviet laboratories were often denied access to certain sites where attempts were allegedly being made to use psychokinesis (PK) – the movement of objects at a distance by mental power alone – in order to induce physical ailments.

Several psychics, notably those who professed the ability to have out-of-body experiences almost to order, told of experiments in 'remote viewing' (in which they tried to see distant places with their minds). These occurred at a science institute in California, funded by the intelligence agencies. Psychics were asked to project themselves to a far location and describe what they saw. This turned out to be a Soviet base already photographed by spy satellites. According to some sources, the psychics performed better than the technology, describing hidden tunnels only discovered much later by conventional means.

Uri Geller subsequently claimed that he was aware of certain experiments in which psychic abilities were used to move distant objects. He was reluctant to talk about these or to discuss the apparently growing military involvement in ESP research.

There is now much debate in the paranormal community about active military development of 'psychotronic' weapons. These combine psychic powers and artificially generated electrical and plasma energy fields that have the potential to produce scrambling effects on the human mind. There are fears that they could be used to create very realistic and terrifying hallucinations (invaluable if directed against an enemy in battle) and that secret testing of such devices might have been responsible for certain recent cases of extraordinary paranormal phenomena. Two

CIA agents approached an American researcher in 1992 to allege that this was happening. They had chosen to break cover and tell the world.

1988 20 JANUARY

'PONG FROM OUTER SPACE'

The Knowles family were driving along the highway from Perth to Adelaide, skirting the Nullarbor Plain on the Western Australia/South Australia border, when their car was allegedly attacked by a strange force.

They observed a light like an egg in a cup twisting on the road ahead, then found themselves underneath it and being sucked upward by its power. Their voices changed in pitch, a vile smell filled the car and a vibration shot through the bodywork. Holding their hands out of the open window in the darkness, two of the occupants felt a spongy object above them but saw nothing. The car then crashed, burst a tyre and slewed to a halt by the roadside.

Upon arrival at the nearest town, Mundrabilla, as dawn broke, they discovered indentations in the car roof and a powdery dust scattered throughout the vehicle. It smelt like bakelite. Driving on for a few hours, they contacted police who vacuumed samples of the dust but could find nothing unusual about it. However, witnesses that morning attest to the family's fear, the driver of another vehicle on the highway describes seeing a mysterious light and others talk of suddenly being buffeted by strong winds.

Theories as to what caused this unusual poltergeist attack (or the 'pong from outer space', as one media source termed it) include an optical mirage of a train on the long, flat stretch of track that runs parallel to the highway for hundreds of miles, or a plasma vortex similar to those that Terence Meaden believes may create crop circles.

125

THE FUTURE BECKONS

As we work our way through the final decade of this incredible century, where do we stand?

The astonishing growth of the freedom movement within eastern Europe that has cleared away old-style Communism has had an intriguing paranormal backlash. Countries formerly under repressive regimes are experiencing a spiritual release that is provoking a dramatic rise in claims of the unexplained.

Strange manifestations, though fewer in number, are supported by more convincing evidence, often on film. Perhaps as a result, there seem to be more scientists showing enthusiasm for the supernatural, prepared to engage in debate, all of which augurs well for the future.

The 1990s

1990

THE SPIRITUAL REVOLUTION

Ex-Beatle and rock star John Lennon, who was murdered ten years earlier, made a dramatic return from death, according to New York psychic Bill Tenuto. Lennon reputedly used his vocal cords to speak messages into a tape recorder, and from 1985 onward was issuing statements about a remarkable series of Earth-changing events that were about to be set in motion.

'Lennon' spoke of a spiritual revolution that would gain momentum in 1989/90 and bring about real peace. He claimed that a team of people in the afterlife calling themselves 'the white brotherhood' (which included, among others, John Wayne!) were doing their utmost at this point in history to alter the world for the better. As 'Lennon' said, 'There will be no more battles, no more wars ... if people want peace they will have peace.'

Opinion is divided within the paranormal community as to whether Lennon's spirit can really be behind these messages. I tried to persuade Cynthia Lennon to hear the tapes but she was understandably reluctant to do so because she felt that some people were abusing her ex-husband's name.

Whatever the case, these words uttered by the New York medium in an impression, at least, of the singer's voice, were documented with me in advance of the events referred to. Exactly coinciding with the timescale proposed, there was indeed a quite unexpected and dramatic spiritual revolution in eastern Europe which, in a matter of months, felled the Berlin wall and ended hard-line Communism in almost all its principal seats of power. This all happened with remarkably little loss of life — a truly peaceful revolution, just as 'Lennon' had predicted.

The peaceful revolution in eastern Europe was allegedly predicted by the spirit of John Lennon.

The late John Wayne is reputedly one of 'the white brotherhood' working for world peace.

1991 10 SEPTEMBER

Whether we have to thank him (and John Wayne) for ending the bitter Cold War and easing the fears of millions of people is likely to be the subject of great controversy that may not be settled until Lennon's spirit makes his (promised) appearance this coming decade on a live TV show!

DOUG AND DAVE'S CROP CIRCLES

Two retired artists from Southampton, Doug Bower and Dave Chorley, usually known affectionately as 'Doug and Dave', revealed in the *Today* newspaper that they had been hoaxing crop circles since 1976. They made them by using a rope and some wood to flatten the crop and had revelled in the invention of ever more fantastic patterns to play games with the experts.

Although some early stories claimed they had made all the circles, this was never the case. Of the 3000 or so markings found between 1980 and 1991, Doug and Dave claim to have made only a couple of hundred, but including the 1980 examples at Westbury, the five circle patterns in 1983 and the pictograms that were decoded as ecological messages in 1989 and 1990. They had now decided to retire and were annoyed by the money cereology was making from their little jest. To prove their case, they claimed to have signed the last dozen circles in summer 1991 with two giant letter 'D's; and, indeed, circles with these letters had clearly been filmed during August. They were thought real!

The artists had a brief flurry with fame, then faded from the scene, after struggling to try to sell a book recounting their exploits. Most serious researchers viewing their evidence accepted that they had made the circles claimed and that copycat hoaxers had followed their work. But hoaxing had been common since the mid-1980s, so this was not a climbdown.

Doug and Dave never professed to have made circles outside southern England, even though they had formed in more than forty countries by the early 1990s. Yet, astonishingly, they were accused by some individuals in the cereology world of being pawns in a government disinformation campaign to destroy the credibility of the phenomenon. The notion that these two men were 'secret agents' (which, frankly, I find absurd) was soon part of circle lore.

Personally, I am satisfied they are sincere, but equally it is important to bear one crucial fact in mind. The day they told their story to the world, I was in the far north Queensland bush of Australia at the site south of Cairns where in January 1966 crop circles had first formed. This was a reedy, poisonous, snake-infested swamp. As I discovered, there had been many other examples here before 1966 and more afterward. Indeed, it is now known that the Aborigines have legends dating back much further. This is a very significant finding, because Doug and Dave admit it was seeing these circles in Australia that gave them the idea to create similar marks in English crop fields after returning home. They are adamant that they did not fake the Queensland circles and, given the deadly snakes that have long inhabited this region, it seems improbable that anybody else did.

Doug and Dave thus fabricated an escalating mystery but modelled it on a real phenomenon — of simple, single circles — that may always have been present worldwide. Single circles are just what researchers such as Paul Fuller argued were left of the phenomenon even before Doug and Dave appeared. They did so because this was the form confirmed by global historical records, described by eye-witnesses in the course of their formation and reproduced artificially in various laboratory experiments when duplicating the environment within a crop field. None were complex patterns.

In other words, the weird formations seem to be a hoax created after 1976 and inspired by Doug and Dave. Yet behind these much publicized shapes were a few genuine examples of simple, unexplained circles that have formed at wide intervals all over the world. Cereology, nevertheless, has survived the crisis. Against the odds, the myth of alien intelligences sending messages in the corn also lives on!

1991 FEBRUARY AND APRIL

UFO VIDEO

A security camera operated by a guard from inside the Birchwood shopping centre complex near Warrington, Cheshire, in northern England, picked up a white globular object about the size of a tennis ball in

26-04-91
00:29:34

Video film of the strange white blob observed at the Warrington shopping centre.

the early hours of the morning. The camera followed this as it climbed walls, circled waste bins and then disappeared. In close focus it resembled a soap bubble. Unwilling to miss anything, the security guard never left his office to visit the site before the object vanished over a tree.

UFO group MUFORA (Manchester UFO Research Association) were called in and invited scientists at the British and Irish Sceptics movement to participate in a unique joint effort to try to solve the case. Could it be film of ball lightning (never before recorded)? Or was there a mundane solution? Luminous insects and optical distortions to the camera lens were debated but no clear answer found. Then, two months later, a different camera observing a second location on the site identified the same thing. This time it was visible for twenty minutes, moving low over a roadway and around a road sign. Again the guard did not leave the building to look for it.

As of late 1993, no other guards claim to have seen the same thing through any of the cameras at the site, although one ex-employee has claimed to have done so when working there, believing it to be an insect. The case remains an intriguing detective puzzle, but unless it was a UFO piloted by very small green men, this is definitely not a film of a spaceship.

1991 27 OCTOBER

GHOST VIDEO

At 4.32 a.m. the burglar alarm from a nightclub in Oldham, Lancashire, in northern England, sounded in the police station. Travelling to the site and meeting the owner, the police discovered no sign of a break-in but noted something quite extraordinary. The security camera had been triggered into action at exactly the time when the alarm sounded. Infra-red beams intercepted by a moving object can do this, but how had the intruder entered the building? When the tape was played back, the answer was amazing. A ghostly, semi-transparent male figure in a white shirt was seen to walk along a corridor past the beams and straight through a closed door as if it was not there!

Unhappily, the video tape was accidentally destroyed before it could reach investigators at ASSAP (Association for the Scientific Study of Anomalous Phenomena) and a copy thus be taken, although still images were secured. Various people who saw it claim it was remarkable evidence.

1992

THE SUPERNATURAL'S STAR RISES IN THE EAST

As the eastern bloc in Europe rushed headlong into democracy, its people began to experience a wave of paranormal events. It was as if the removal of repression that had outlawed support for such things had opened a gate and released a torrent from within the psyche of these cultures.

In countries such as Romania there were frequent sightings of angels. One astonishing episode was reported during a space mission planned by the former USSR, when cosmonauts claimed to have seen a glowing winged creature materialize briefly inside their sealed capsule far above the Earth's surface.

Religion throughout the former Communist states had been heavily restricted and spiritual beliefs were widely frowned upon. However, the soul of a nation could not be suppressed and worship had continued regardless of the persecution that sometimes resulted. Some thought that the new freedom was expressing itself as a dramatic outburst of hallucinatory experiences which had been bottled up for decades. Others felt that these angelic visions were a sign that the overthrow of Communism had met with divine favour.

Crop circles also made their way into eastern Europe. They were discovered in Russia, Georgia and Latvia, with particularly bizarre patterns near Bucharest in Romania. In May and June 1992, Hungary became the latest centre of activity when a series of single circles, aligned like planets in a solar system, appeared south of Budapest. Several weeks later, however, two youths came forward to explain that they had faked two single circles with a piece of wood. In just a few days, Hungary went through what Britain had taken ten years to experience.

Hungary was also the focal point for some intriguing cases of spacenapping. The victims were young, aged between 18 and 25, and from professional categories, including a nurse and a pilot.

In one incident in January 1992, near Szeksvard, a woman found her car dumped into a field surrounded by untouched snow that had fallen several days before. She only recalled seeing a strange light before the transportation.

Another woman saw an object land beside her house and developed odd markings on her abdomen. She was found to be pregnant and an ultrasound revealed the foetus, but upon the next check, and without her having suffered a miscarriage, the ultrasound revealed that she was no longer pregnant.

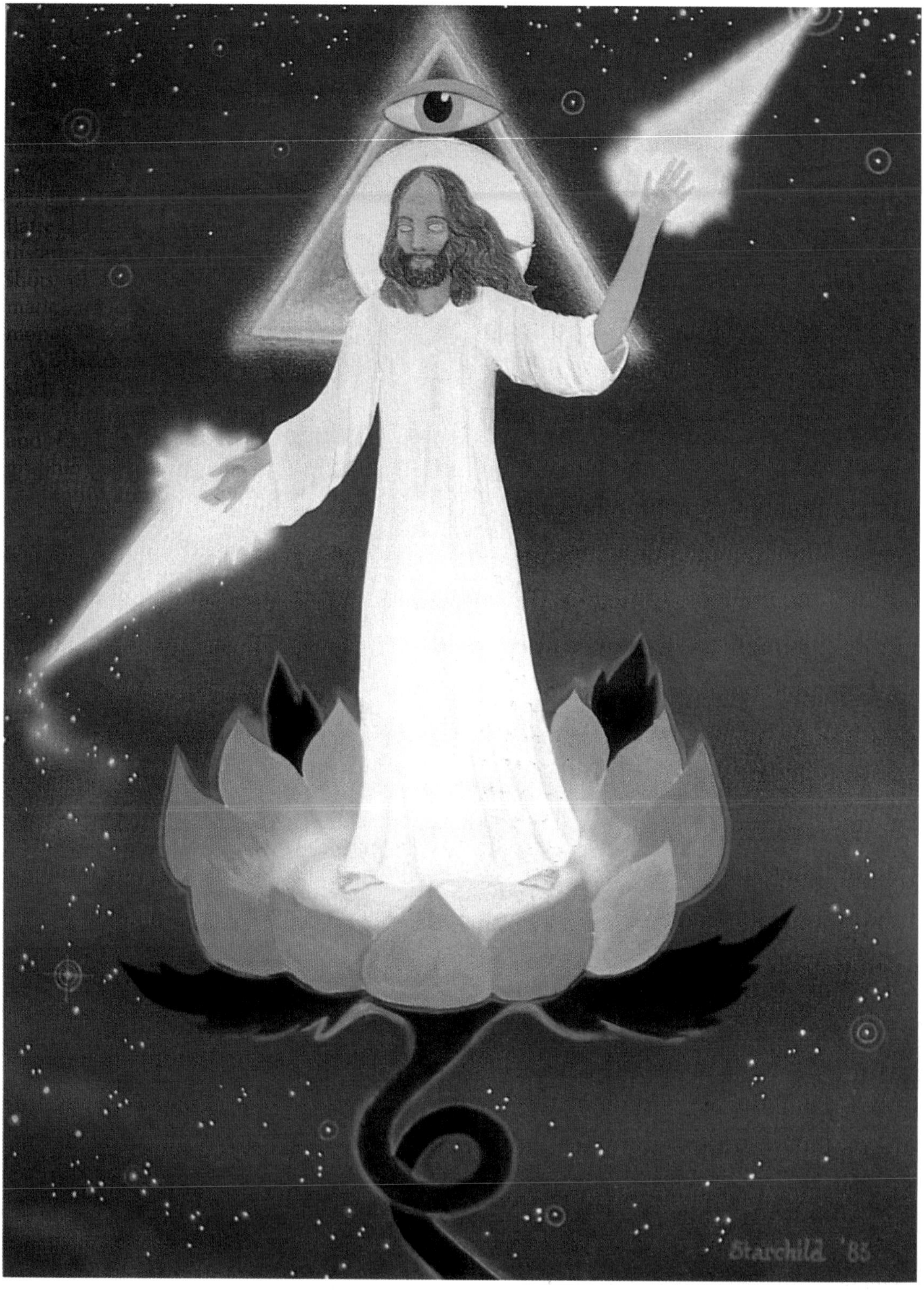
Starchild '85

Left: an interpretation of angelic visions by Judith Starchild.
Above: a Hungarian town noted for strange phenomena.

In December 1992, several former members of the old Academy of Sciences in Moscow got together to launch eastern Europe's first privately funded research project into strange phenomena. Given the success of Soviet experiments during the 1960s in fields such as Kirlian energy, psychokinesis and ESP, the creation of this body — called Aura Z — could be a significant step forward.

1992 JUNE

MASS SPACENAPPING

The Roper organization conducted the biggest-ever poll to survey how many American citizens had symptoms that could be suggestive of a spacenapping. Features sought were missing periods of memory, odd recurrent dreams and phobias about certain locations, often involving major detours to avoid taking the quickest route without any understanding of the reason.

It was expected that perhaps one in a thousand people might emerge as possible abductees, but the results were staggering. Almost five million Americans were diagnosed as potential victims of a spacenapping. The vast majority had no memory of this.

A major six-day symposium was organized at the prestigious Massachusetts Institute of Technology (MIT) by physicist Dr David Pritchard, and the highly respected psychologist, Dr John Mack, based at adjacent Harvard University. Experts from all over the world examined every facet of the spacenapping mystery and concluded that there was a significant global problem of extraordinary proportions. The popular theory that abductees are 'fantasy prone personalities' was rejected after a series of test results that were premiered here by psychologists.

1993 JUNE

THE REINCARNATION OF MARY SUTTON

Perhaps the most remarkable case yet of reincarnation emerged this month with the revelations by Jenny Cockell from Northamptonshire, central England, in her book *Yesterday's Children.* Jenny claimed that from early childhood she was plagued by strange dreams of a woman in a cottage, a violent husband and a large family of children. She had a sense of unfinished business and an urge to find out more.

Eventually, despite marrying and trying to forget, she could not escape the pressure of this weird alter ego that kept intruding into her dreams. She had so much information about this other life that she was able to sketch the layout of a village that she knew instinctively was in Ireland.

Finally, Jenny obtained detailed maps of the area north of Dublin where she was convinced this other woman had lived. Examining the Malahide area, she discovered that her dream memories matched exactly with this location and that they related to twenty-five years prior to her own birth.

Travelling to Ireland, many of her sketches came to life. She knew the town, had drawn its buildings from her dream 'memory' and was able to locate the derelict cottage where the long-dead woman of her dreams had actually lived. That woman was named Mary Sutton and after her death at a young age her large family of children had been split apart and sent to various foster homes. They never saw one another again.

Jenny was convinced that she retained these memories because she had to compensate for this tragedy. If she was indeed the reincarnation of Mary Sutton, it could be that these images were pouring out of her subconscious because 'her' early death fifty years previously somehow had now to be set right.

After considerable effort, Jenny Cockell was able to track down several of 'her' surviving children and bring them all together for an astonishing reunion in the house they all once shared. They had been apart for much of their lives. Yet they were staggered by the intimate details of their childhood that this woman could provide. How could she know so much? But was Jenny Cockell, years younger than any of them, really their mother? They wondered if, instead, the dead mother they remembered was speaking through her from heaven in order to bring the family together again for one last time.

In October 1993 Jenny Cockell told me that she was now researching further dreams and memories emerging under hypnosis. These told of a future life in the twenty-first century where she knows 'tomorrow's children' – yet to be born.

1993 JULY

STRANGE ENERGIES

Andy Collins launched a major new study into the mysterious phenomenon of 'orgone' energy. First isolated by controversial American researcher Wilhelm Reich, it was supposed to be a biological force akin to ectoplasm and body electricity but which survived in the atmosphere as a living thing and could be 'charged' for good or evil from other living forms.

Reich's experiments attempted to scatter clouds by dispersing energy through strange-looking guns. But he was pursued by military authorities and dogged by other problems. His work was largely forgotten, save for its encapsulation in the hit song 'Cloudbusting', written by Kate Bush.

Collins believed that this force in the atmosphere might be responsible for both UFOs and crop circles. It was largely invisible, but interacted with, and depended upon, human consciousness. It might build

Wilhelm Reich's orgone box.

a bridge between the natural plasma energies that cautious researchers were supporting and the 'unknown intelligence' that many others argued must be behind the unexplained phenomena both of crop circles and spacenappings.

Perhaps the plasma was orgone energy and the intelligence ourselves. Other researchers had speculated about 'living animals' in the atmosphere which were nor-

mally invisible but could be filmed by means of infra-red photography. It was certainly true that crop circle researchers were frequently finding strange 'blobs' on photographs taken at sites where nothing had been visible at the time. Investigations of 'window' areas after unusual phenomena in the vicinity had also revealed similar

Bust of Wilhelm Reich, with his cloudbuster, at Rangeley, Maine, USA.

MYSTERY FACE ON MARS

During the close-survey probes that orbited Mars in 1976, something very strange was photographed in the Cydonia region. The Viking probe filmed it twice, in July and August, from different orbital positions. While NASA laughed it off as a trick of light and shade, an accidental effect seemed unlikely because of the varied lighting conditions that prevailed for these multiple images, shot from different angles and at different times.

The photographs appeared to show a human face, with eyes, nose and mouth, measuring a mile in diameter. Later work by computer specialists enhanced details and, rather than destroying the illusion as would have been likely had this been an optical trick, they revealed new features, such as eyeballs.

The debate has raged ever since. Was this a monument erected on the Martian surface by a long-dead civilization? Or, given that it was too small to be seen by any telescope on Earth, was it placed there to resemble us and so attract our attention, only being detectable when our technology proved capable of visiting Mars? Perhaps it was a calling card left long ago by alien visitors to our solar system — the ET equivalent of 'Kilroy was here'.

Sadly, NASA seemed reluctant to take new photographs with more sophisticated cameras. However, lobbying by several scientists and through the United Nations achieved this promise. A probe was launched in 1992 and in September 1993 was due to return photographs of Cydonia which would have ended the dispute. Either they would have proved this to be merely a rock that cast shadows and chanced to resemble a human face or the artificial nature of the 'monument' would have been undeniable. Meanwhile the mystery remains.

unseen masses on site pictures. Were these examples of orgone energy briefly visible to the sensitivity of the film or simply unnoticed by the eyes of the camera operator?

Collins mounted a project in the Woodborough Hill area near Alton Barnes, Wiltshire, in southern England, during July 1993. Several impressive crop circles had formed here and there were numerous accounts of strange lights being seen. His team used 'cloudbusting' equipment to try to trigger orgone energy into life and photographed the proceedings with infra-red film. Enough unusual images did appear to warrant further study.

While opinion is divided as to how relevant this work may be to UFOs or crop circles, there is no doubt that, as has happened so often in the past, Andy Collins has set a new trend in motion and that as the 1990s progress, the quest for orgone energy will hot up.

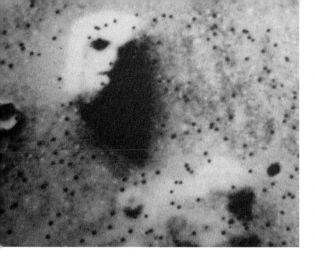

The strange face on the surface of Mars. A trick of the light or the work of an alien intelligence?

Yet, as the probe ended its year-long trek through space and was about to enter parking orbit and begin its mission, all contact with it was lost. NASA — having expended huge sums on its various experiments — was distraught. Nobody knew whether it had suffered a simple malfunction, was actually taking its photographs and unable to return them to Earth, or failing to respond to NASA's instructions. Equally likely, it could have been hit by a meteor and destroyed. Or, as some researchers were not slow to point out, maybe the aliens had silenced it!

In any case, it had vanished, as had the chance of resolving the fascinating mystery of the Martian face for at least several more years.

Of course, rumours soon began to circulate that photographs had been returned to Earth and did conclusively prove that the face was an alien construction. But why would NASA hide such a fascinating fact? Naturally this has all been denied. So the mystery lives on.

1993 2 SEPTEMBER

HAUNTED TECHNOLOGY

The paranormal is an ongoing process. There will always be new cases to report and new trends to describe.

The previously mentioned examples of video-recorded UFOs and ghosts are by no means unique. In August 1993, no fewer than six new cases of odd things captured by camcorder were brought to my immediate notice. This is certain to be a major factor in coming investigations.

Another intriguing variation is the allegation that technology is being 'hijacked' by some intelligent force to create new mysteries — a real ghost in the machine. If I were to don my Nostradamus hat, this would be my prophecy for the paranormal mystery that will dominate the 1990s.

There have been claims that TV sets have transmitted strange voices when all stations have gone off the air; in one case, a witness swears he saw the image of his dead dog appear on screen this way. Video tape recorders left on overnight should record nothing but static yet have reportedly received fuzzy images from unknown sources. So far these have been nothing that could not be explained as a freak reception of another TV channel.

There have even been cases of spectrally affected inanimate objects, such as a telephone answerphone that was 'possessed' and a vacuum cleaner that replayed sounds as if it had recorded them — the sounds seeming to be those of the factory staff who built it or the shopkeeper who had sold it!

On 2 September 1993, the latest variation occurred in Dublin. A young couple had bought a baby alarm system that broadcast signals from the nursery to any room in the house where the wireless receiver was carried. All went well until the device began to emit cries from a child who was not there, plus screams and music. Noises like machinery then emerged and eventually the alarm drifted into a static hiss and resumed normal working. Was this a radio station or signals from another alarm system picked up by freak atmospheric effects? Or are baby alarms the latest in a long line of objects to become haunted during this most mysterious of centuries?

and onward ...

W ho knows what a review of the twenty-first century, decade by decade, will one day have to tell us? It is safe to predict that some of the things that are discussed in this book will be accepted as scientific fact and taught in our schools, others rejected as a passing fancy. A few, no doubt, will still be debated together with new mysteries that are bound to crop up.

We live in a changing Universe and are constantly learning amazing new things about it. The paranormal is but a name that we give to the surf that rides the current taking us day by day into the future.

The Earth as seen from space. Are we alone or are we being watched?

FURTHER READING

The following books by no means form an exhaustive list of titles that discuss some of the cases featured in this volume, but they are particularly useful.

Andrews, Colin and Delgado, Pat, *Circular Evidence*, Bloomsbury, 1989

Barry, James, *Ball Lightning and Bead Lightning*, Plenum, 1980

Baxter, John and Atkins, Thomas, *The Fire Came By*, Doubleday, 1976

Begg, Paul, *Into Thin Air*, David & Charles, 1979

Berlitz, Charles, *The Bermuda Triangle*, Doubleday, 1974

Bernstein, Morey, *The Search for Bridey Murphy*, Hutchinson, 1956

Blackmore, Sue, *Beyond the Body*, Heinemann, 1982
           Dying to Live, Grafton, 1993

Bord, Janet and Colin, *Alien Animals*, Grafton, 1981

Chatelain, Maurice, *Our Ancestors Came from Outer Space*, Doubleday, 1978

Clark, Jerome, *The UFO Encyclopedia* (three vols), Omnigraphics, 1990, 1992, 1994

Cockell, Jenny, *Yesterday's Children*, Piatkus, 1993

Collins, Andy, *The Circle Makers*, ABC Books, 1992
           The Seventh Sword, Century, 1992

Condon, Edward, ed., *Scientific Study of UFOs*, Bantam, 1969

Constable, Trevor, *The Cosmic Pulse of Life*, Merlin, 1976

Davies, Paul, *Other Worlds*, Dent, 1980

Doyle, Arthur Conan, *The Coming of the Fairies*, Doran, 1922

Däniken, Erich von, *Chariots of the Gods?*, Souvenir Press, 1969

Devereux, Paul, *Earthlights*, Turnstone, 1982
           Earthlights Revelation, Blandford, 1989

Francis, Di, *Cat Country*, David & Charles, 1983

Fuller, John, *The Interrupted Journey*, Putnam, 1966 (updated Souvenir Press, 1980)
           The Ghost of 29 Megacycles, Grafton, 1987

Geller, Uri and Playfair, Guy, *The Geller Effect*, Souvenir Press, 1989

Harris, Melvin, *Sorry You've Been Duped*, Weidenfeld & Nicolson, 1986

Heuvelmans, Bernard, *On the Track of Unknown Animals*, Hill & Wang, 1958

Hoagland, Richard, *The Monuments of Mars*, North Atlantic Press, 1987

Hough, Peter and Randles, Jenny, *Spontaneous Human Combustion*, Robert Hale, 1992

Jung, Carl, *Flying Saucers: A Modern Myth*, Routledge & Kegan Paul, 1959

Kagan, Daniel and Summers, Ian, *Mute Evidence,* Bantam, 1984

Keatman, Martin and Phillips, Graham, *The Green Stone,* Spearman, 1982

Keyhoe, Donald, *Flying Saucers Are Real,* Holt, 1950

Kusche, Larry, *The Bermuda Triangle: Mystery Solved,* Harper & Row, 1975

Leslie, Desmond and Adamski, George, *Flying Saucers Have Landed,* Laurie, 1953

Lunan, Duncan, *Man and the Stars,* Souvenir Press, 1974

Machen, Arthur, *The Bowmen and Other Legends of the War,* 1915 (his work published as *Tales of the Supernatural,* Grafton, 1975)

Mackal, Roy, *A Living Dinosaur?,* Brill, 1987

Moody, Raymond, *Life After Life,* Bantam, 1975

Moore, Bill and Berlitz, Charles, *The Philadelphia Experiment,* Grafton, 1979

Moss, Thelma, *The Probability of the Impossible,* Paladin, 1979

Moulton Howe, Linda, *An Alien Harvest,* Littleton, 1989

Nickell, Joe and Fischer, John, *Secrets of the Supernatural,* Prometheus, 1988

Oberg, James, *UFOs and Outer Space Mysteries,* Donning, 1982

Persinger, Michael and Lafreniere, Ghyslaine, *Space-time Transients and Unusual Events,* Nelson-Hall, 1977

Randles, Jenny, *UFOs and How to See Them,* Anaya, 1992
From Out of the Blue, Berkley, 1993

Randles, Jenny and Fuller, Paul, *Crop Circles: A Mystery Solved,* Robert Hale, 1990 (updated 1993)

Randles, Jenny and Hough, Peter, *Death by Supernatural Causes?,* Grafton, 1988

Randles, Jenny and Warrington, Peter, *Science and the UFOs,* Basil Blackwell, 1985

Raudive, Konstantin, *Breakthrough,* Smythe, 1971

Rhine, J.B., *The Reach of the Mind,* Pelican, 1954

Ridpath, Ian, *Messages from the Stars,* Futura, 1978

Ring, Ken, *The Omega Project,* William Morrow, 1992

Sheldrake, Rupert, *A New Science of Life,* Blond & Briggs, 1981

Story, Ronald, *The Space Gods Revealed,* NEL, 1977

Strand, Erling, *Project Hessdalen: Final Technical Report,* Project, Hessdalen, 1985

Temple, Robert, *The Sirius Mystery,* Souvenir Press, 1976

Watson, Lyall, *Supernature,* Hodder & Stoughton, 1975

Wilson, Ian, *Mind Out of Time,* Gollancz, 1981

Witchell, Nicholas, *The Loch Ness Story,* Penguin, 1975 (updated 1991)

INDEX

ACKNOWLEDGEMENTS

The author wishes to thank the following for their advice and assistance:

Keith Basterfield, Janet Bord, Bill Chalker, Jerome Clark, David Clarke, Andy
Collins, Paul Devereux, Paul Fuller, Peter Hough, Cynthia Hinde, Kevin
McClure, Bill Moore, Andy Roberts, Malcolm Robinson, Vic Sleigh, 'Doc' Shiels,
Roy Sandbach, Jim Templeton, Nigel Watson.

The author and publishers would like to thank the following for the use of their
photographs:

Mary Evans Picture Library: 10, 13, 17, 18-19, 22, 23, 24, 38, 45, 51, 69 (bottom),
70, 72, 77, 81, 92, 96; Fate Magazine, 43; Fortean Picture Library, frontispiece, 6,
12, 16, 21, 25, 30, 35, 39, 54, 55, 59, 83, 91, 98, 100-1, 104 (bottom), 105, 108,
122, 124, 135, 136; John Gilbert, 37; Images Colour Library, 11, 29, 32, 33, 40
(bottom), 48, 49, 93, 100 (left), 138; Tony McMunn, 75; Pictorial Press, 127, 128;
Popperfoto, 7, 28, 71; St Petersburg, Florida, Police, 74; Roy Sandbach, 112, 120;
Science Photo Library, 88, 89; Judith Starchild, 133.

Every effort has been made to trace the copyright holders of the photographs in
this book. If we have failed to credit the correct copyright holder in any instance
we would be delighted to set the matter right in future editions if the correct
source is brought to our attention.